SWEAR WORDS
COLORING BOOK FOR ADULTS

THIS FUNNY
COLORING BOOK
BELONGS TO:

....

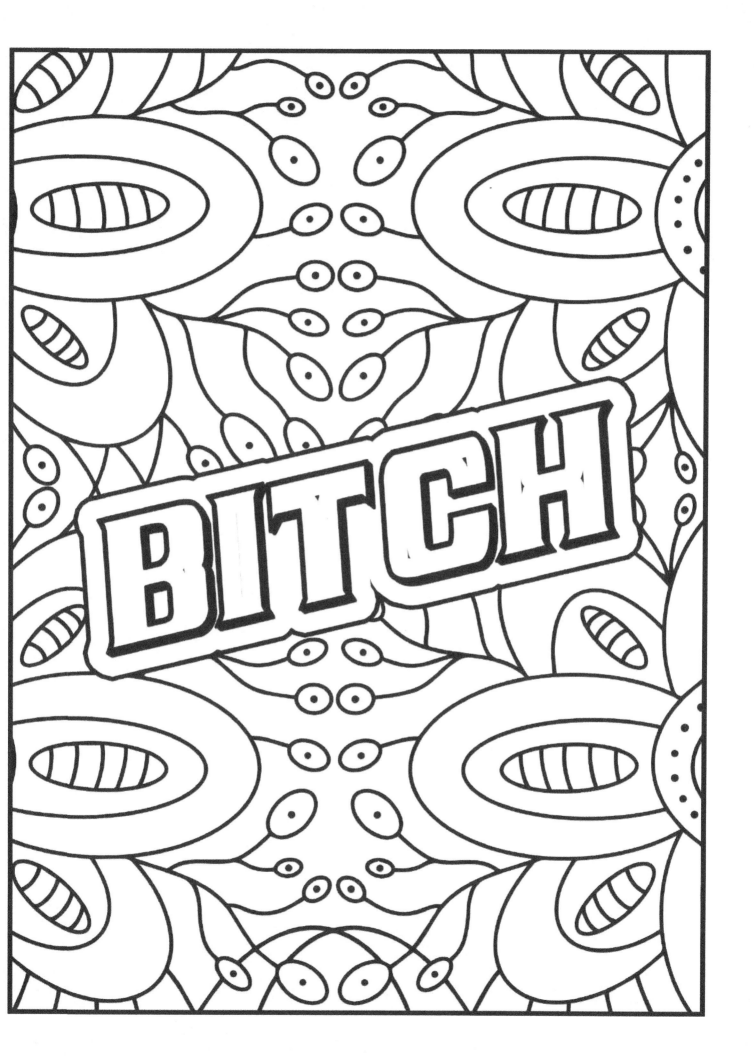

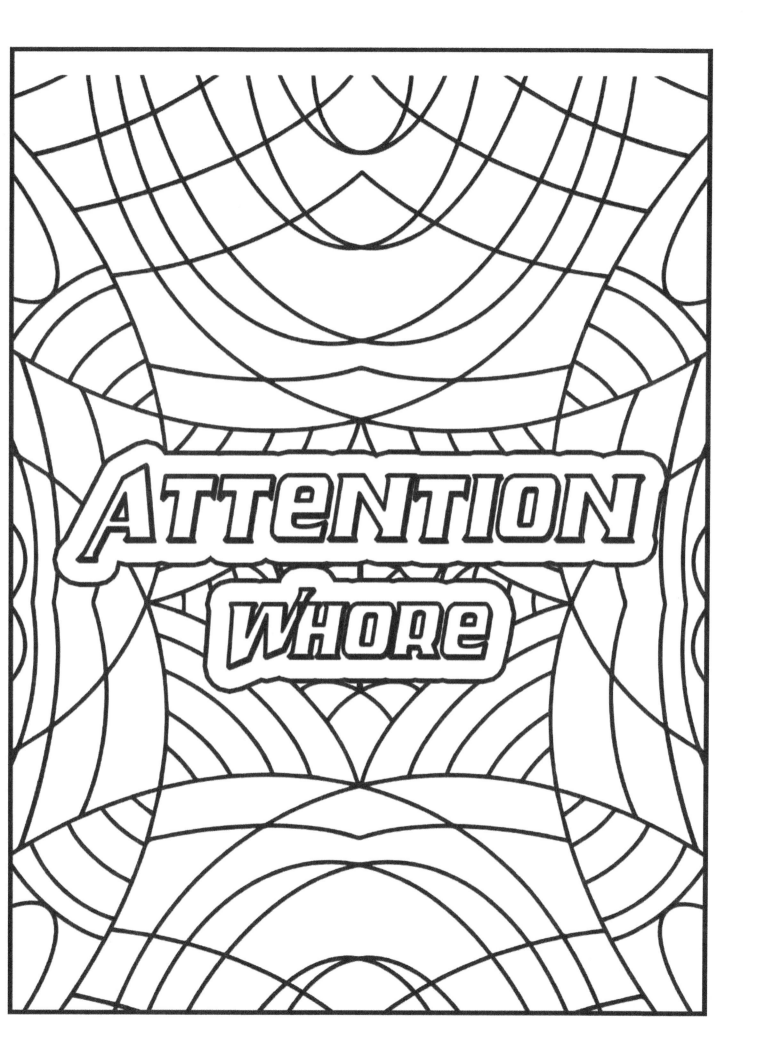

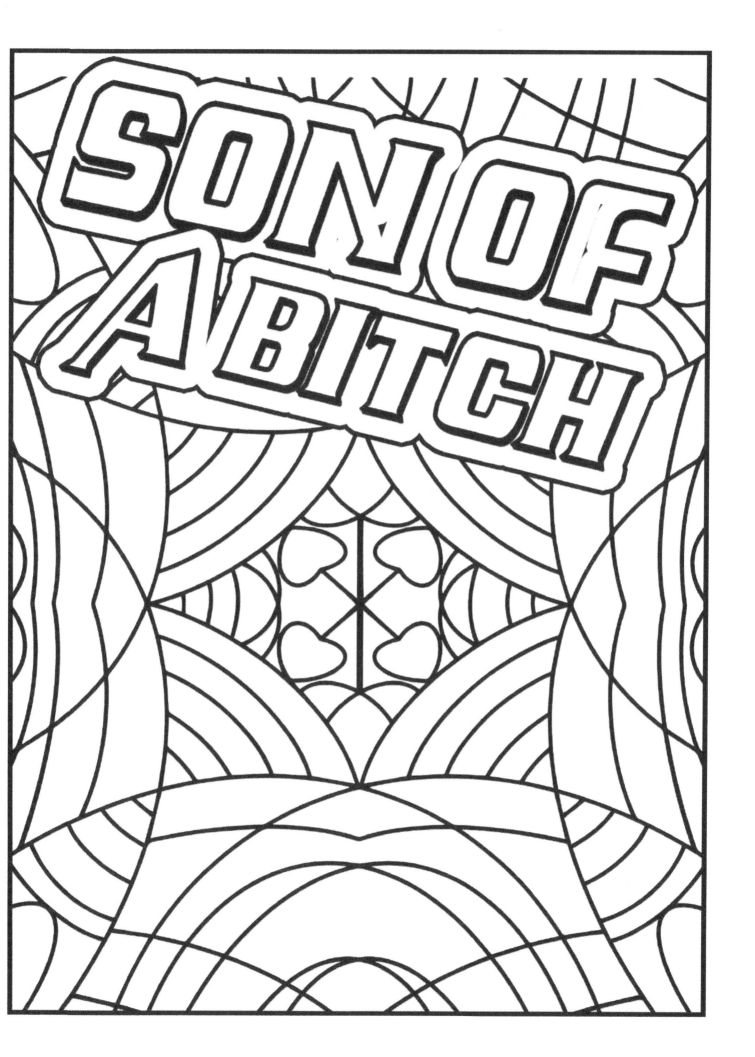

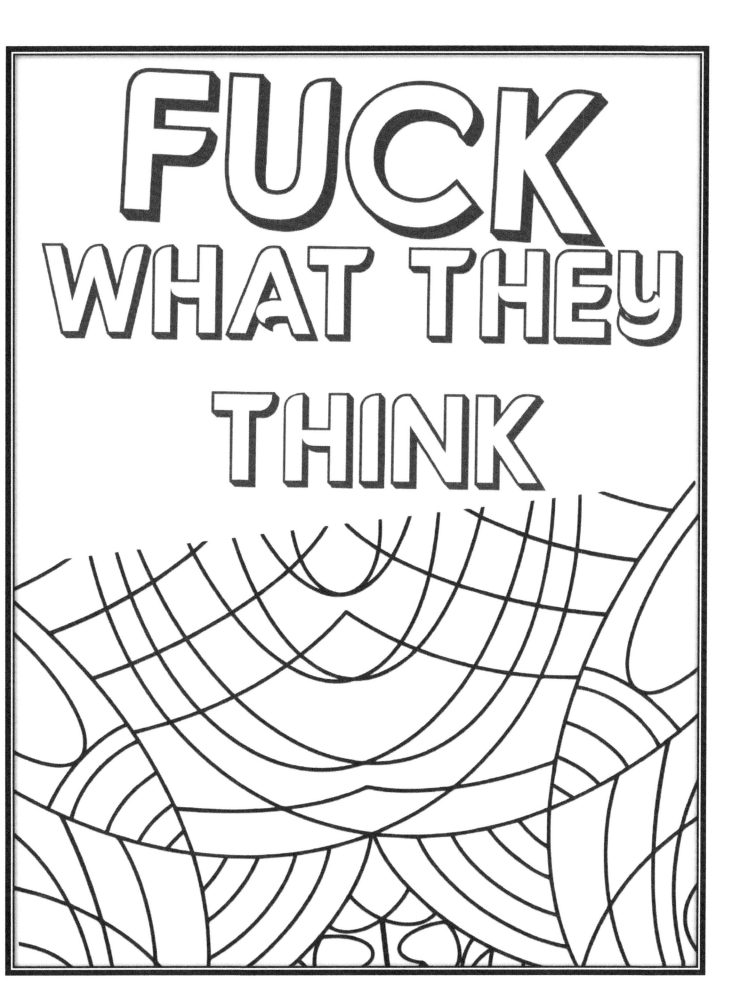

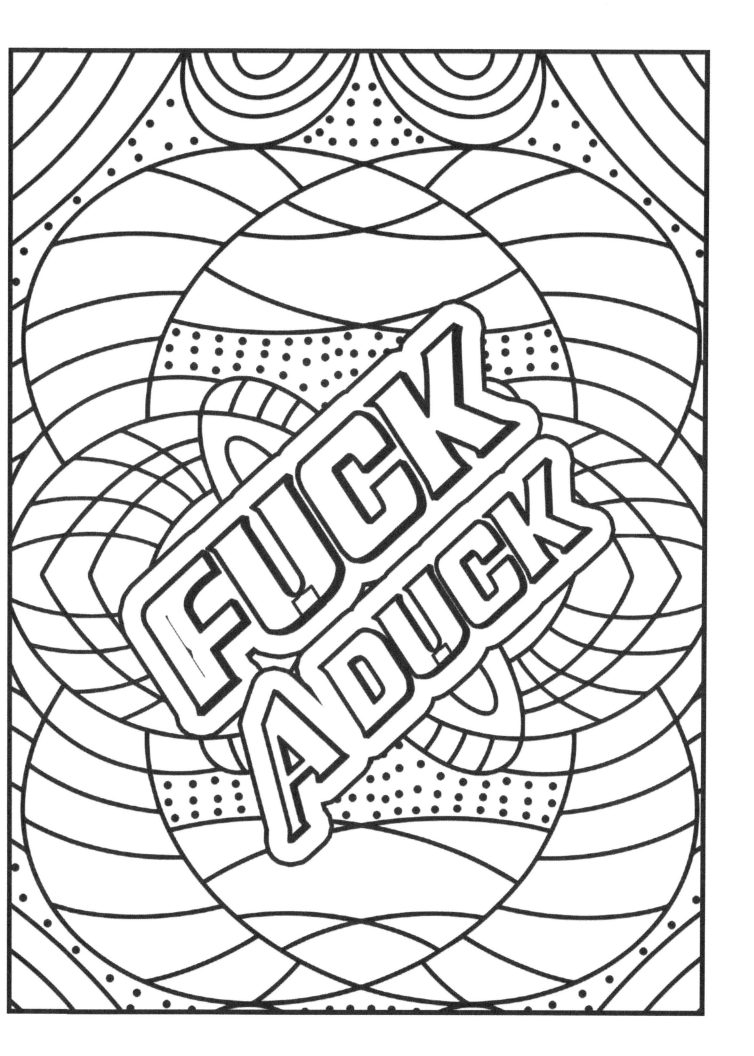

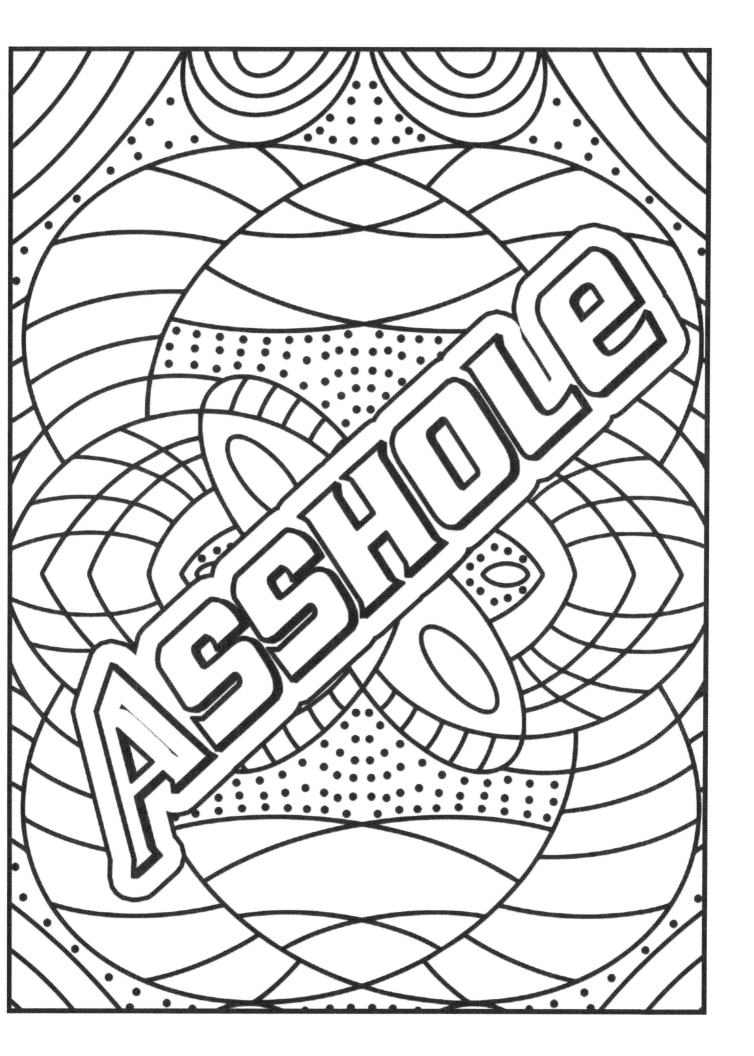

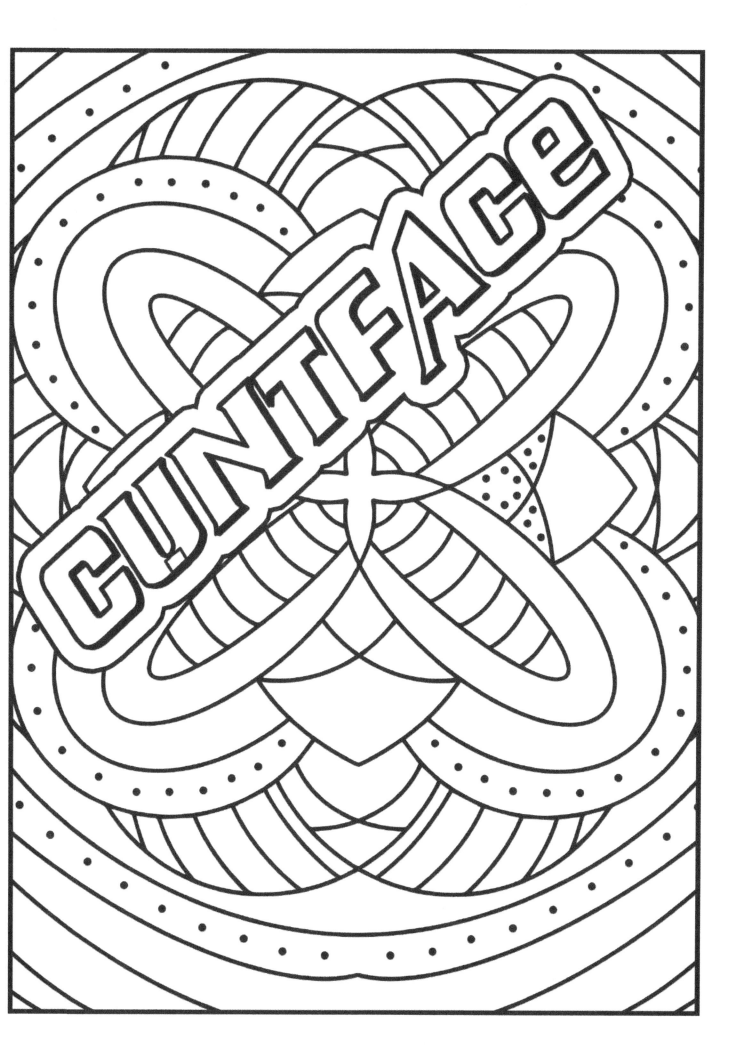

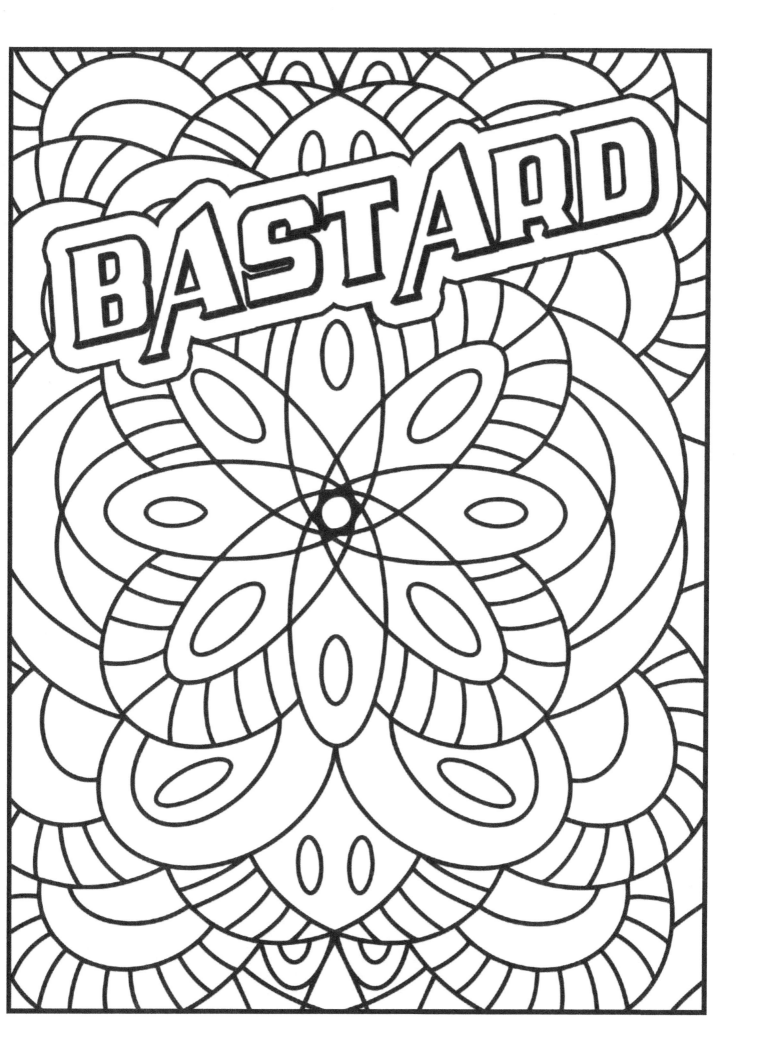

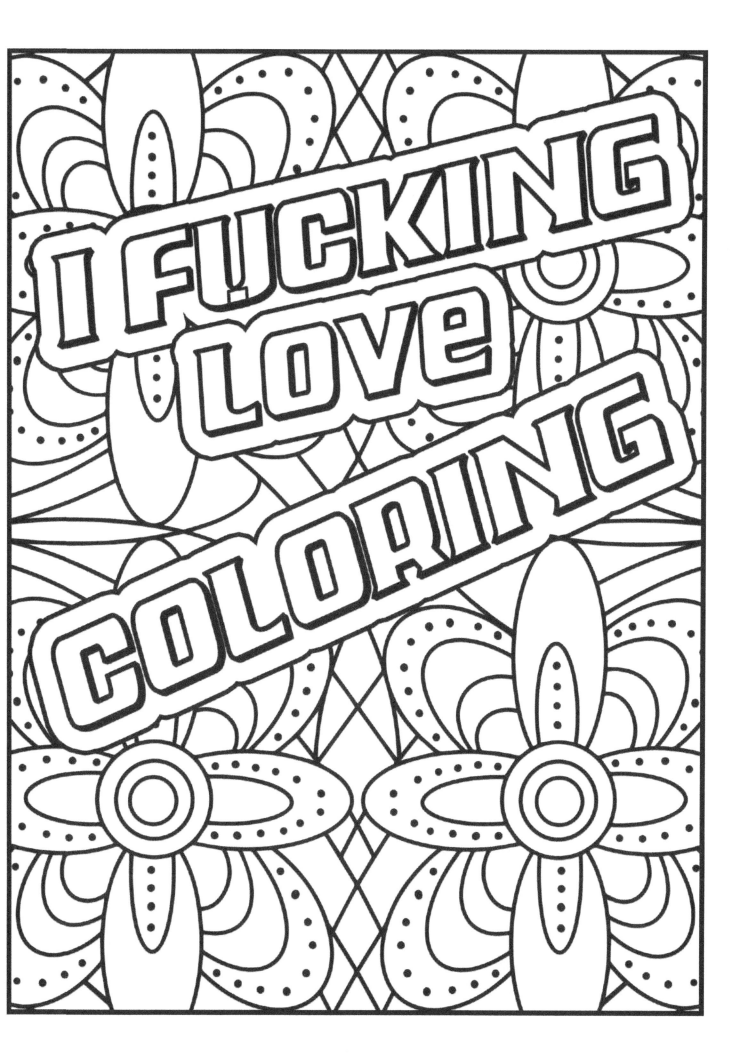

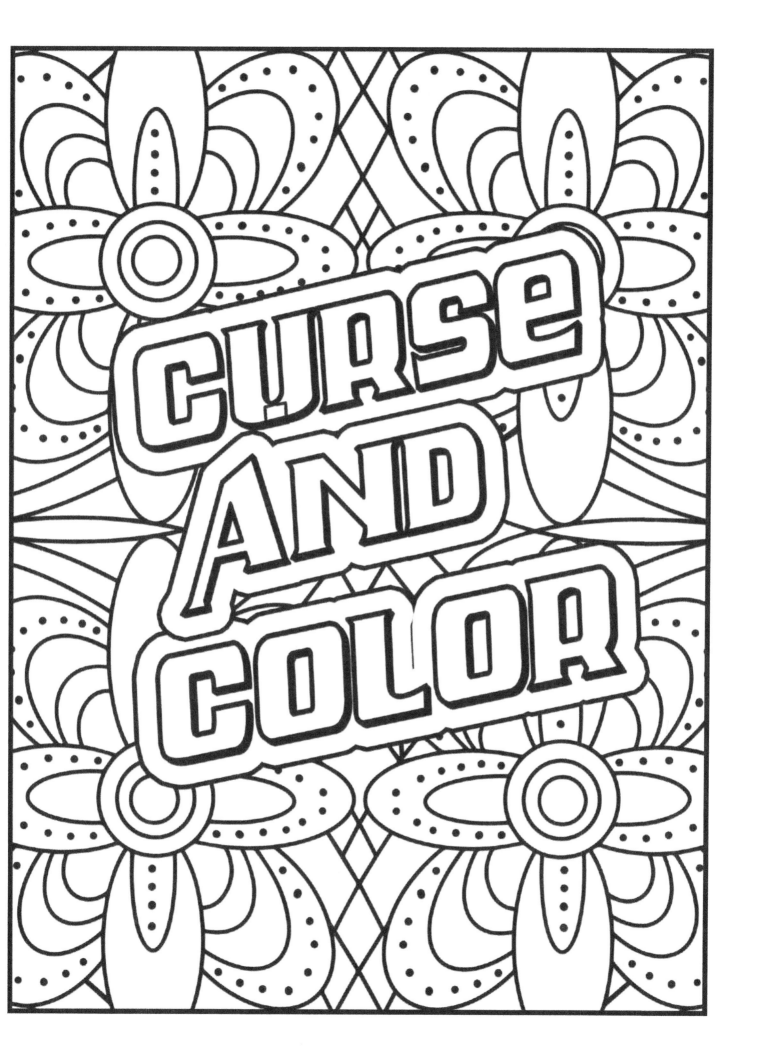

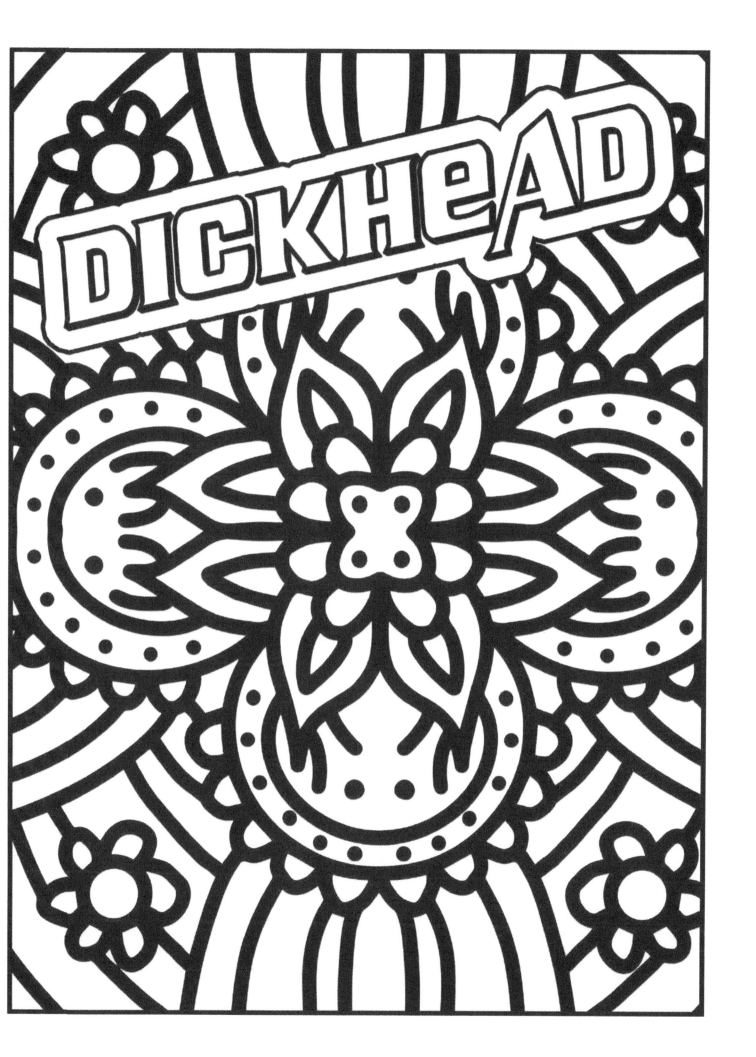

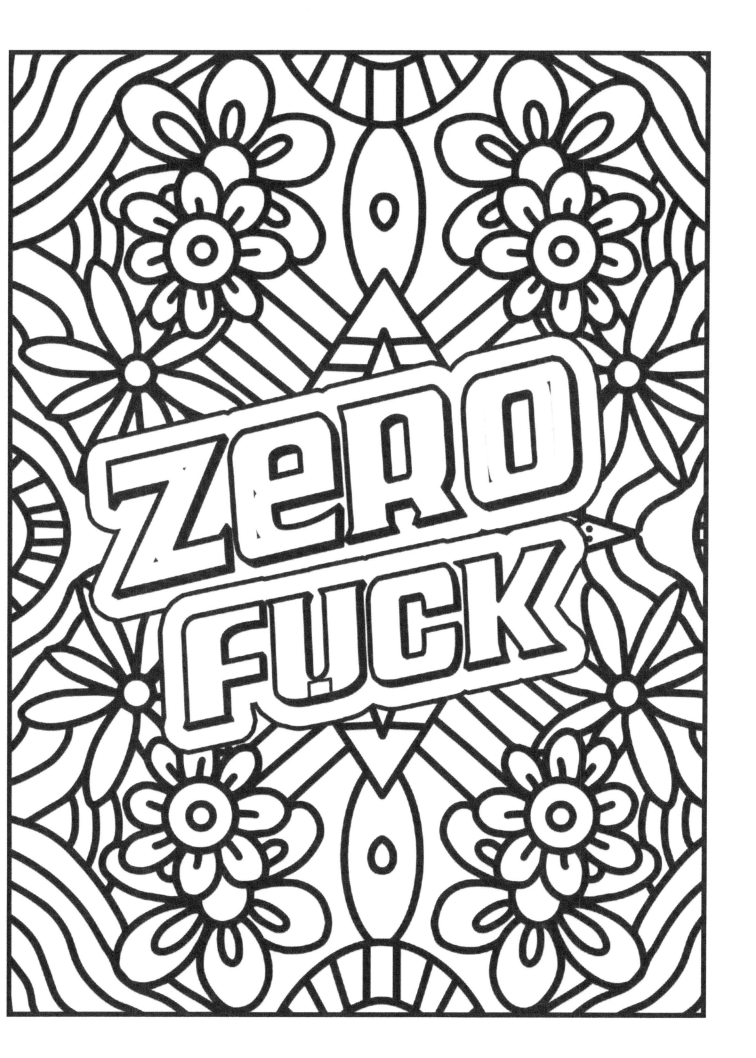

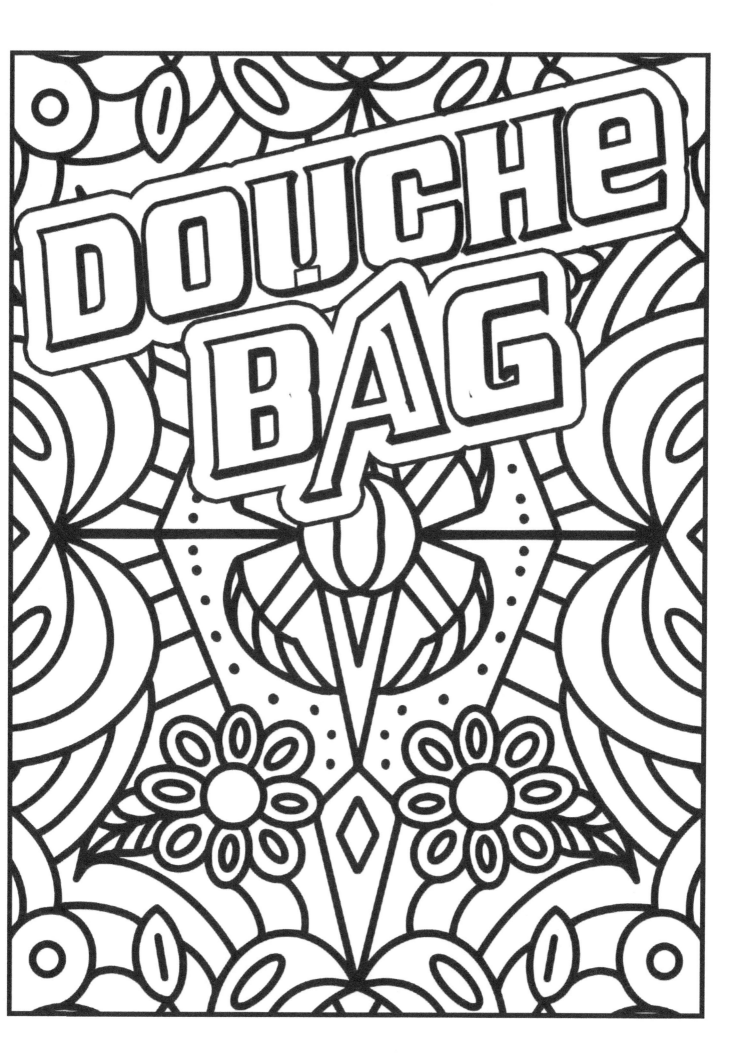

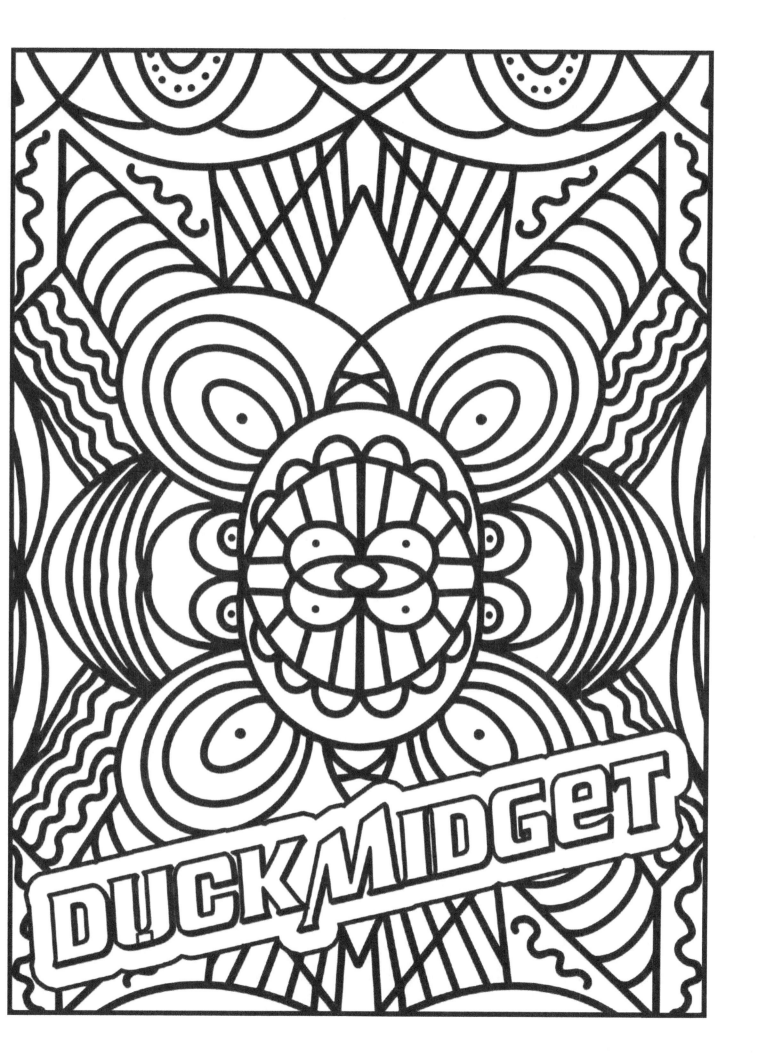

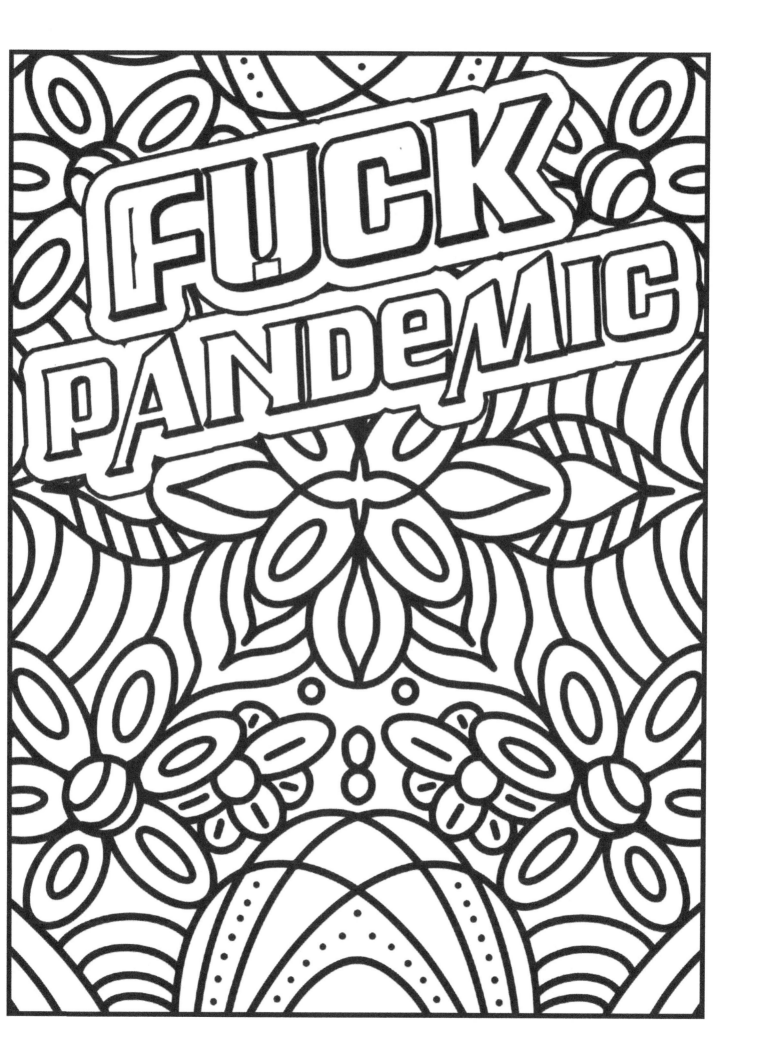

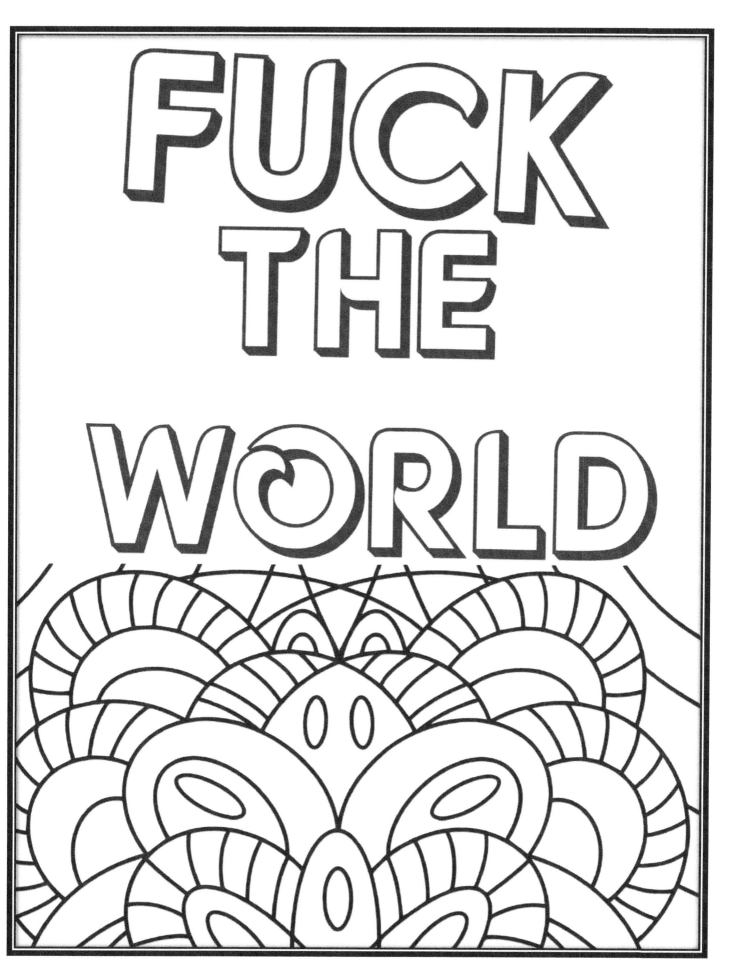

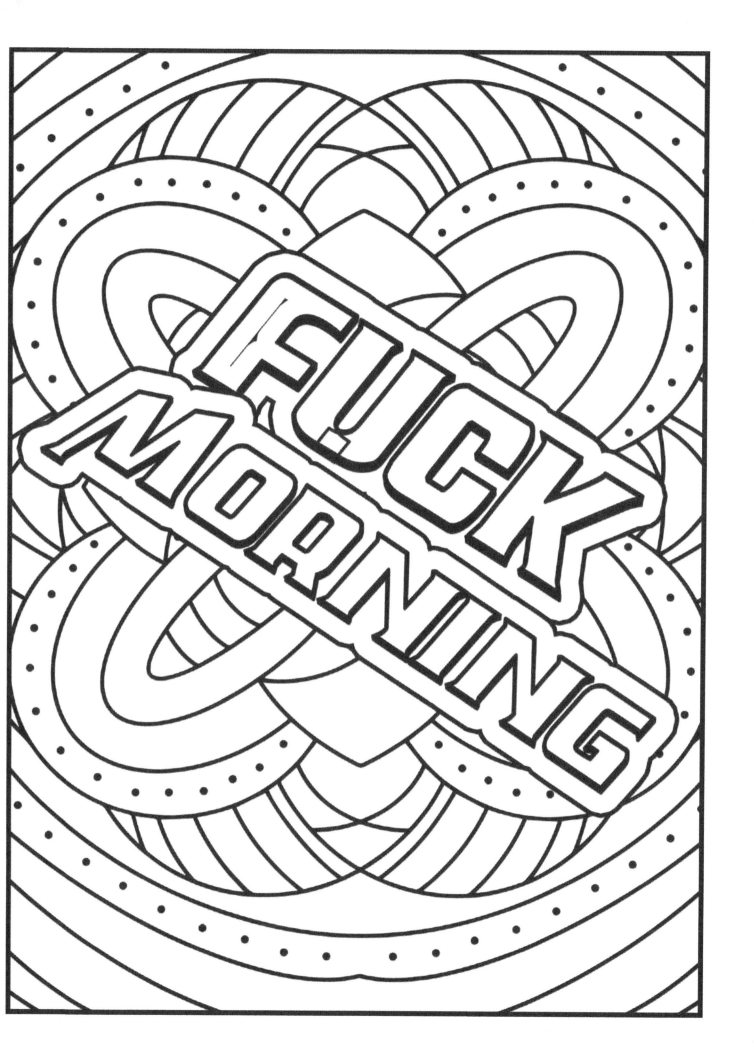

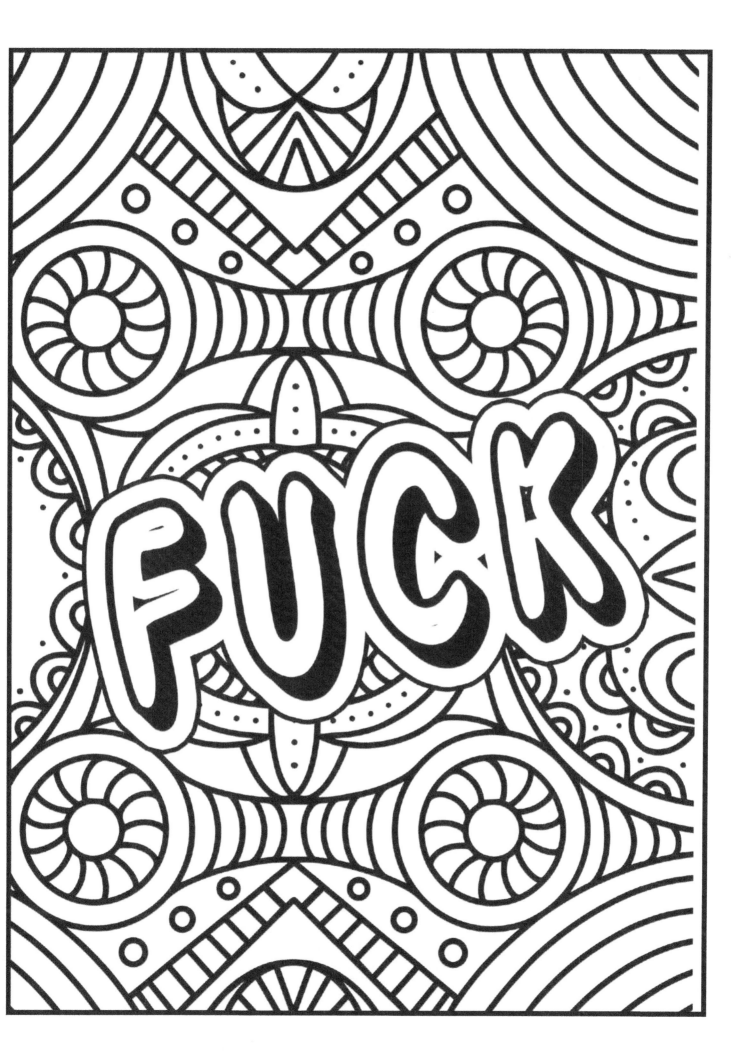

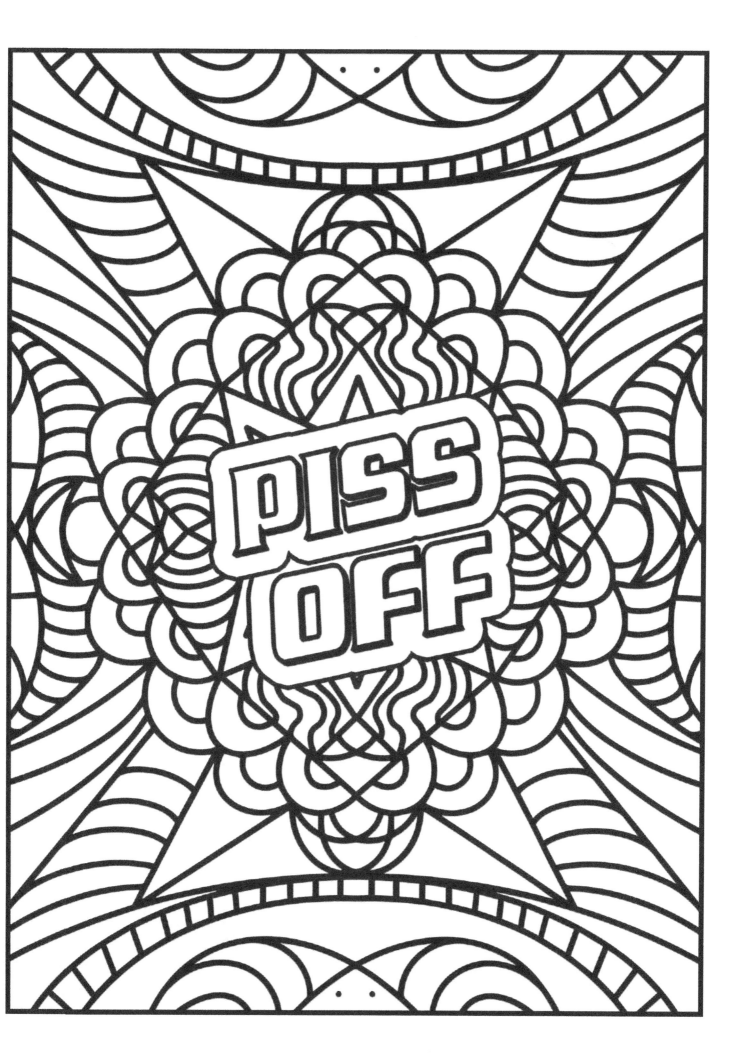

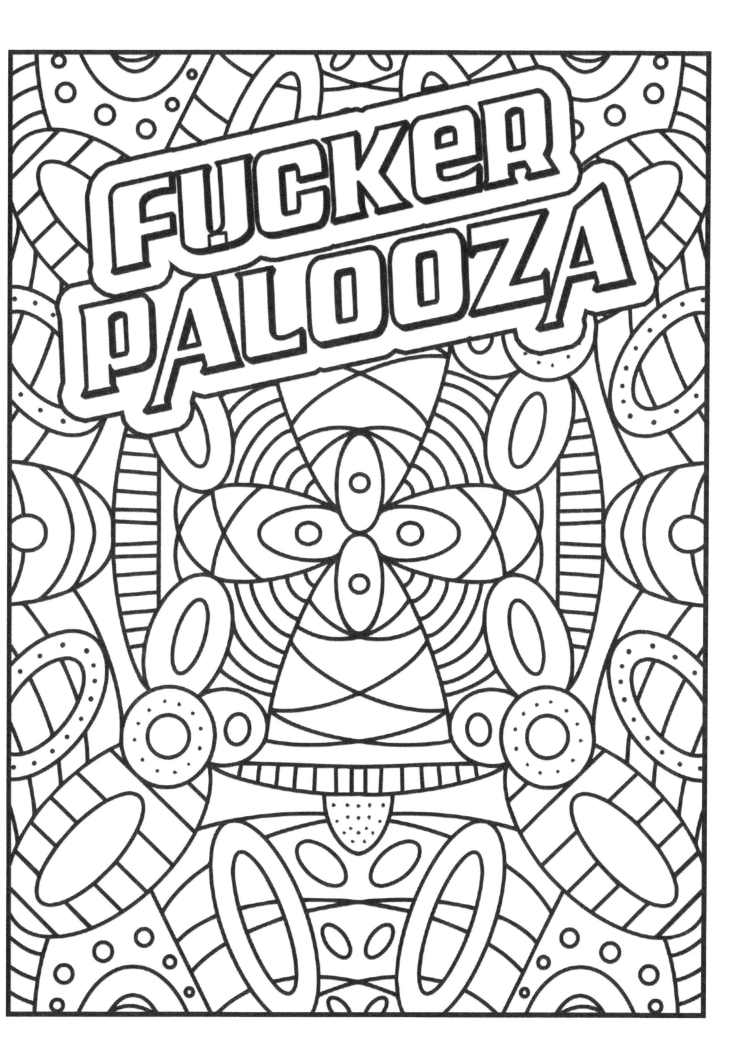

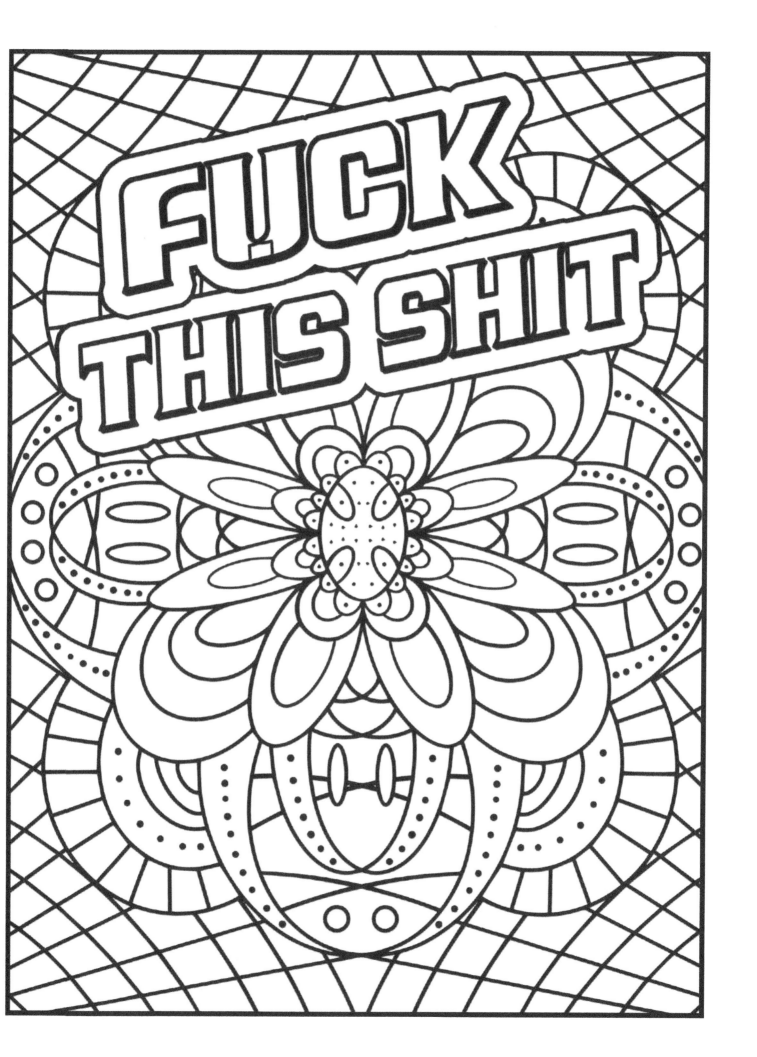

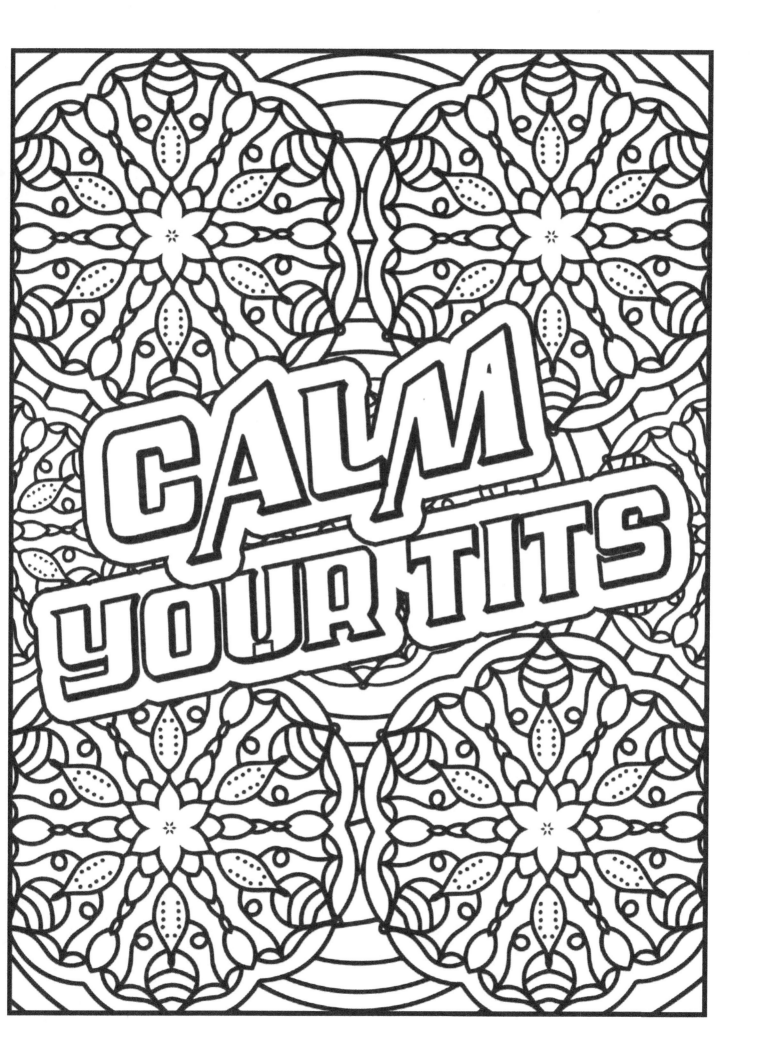

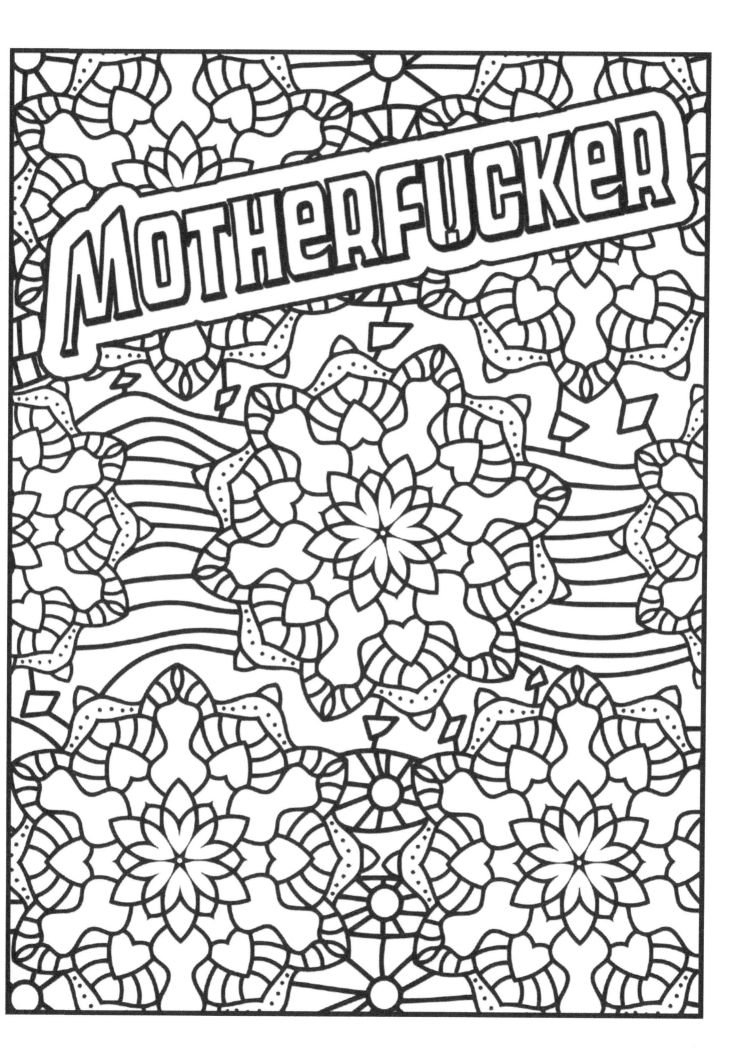

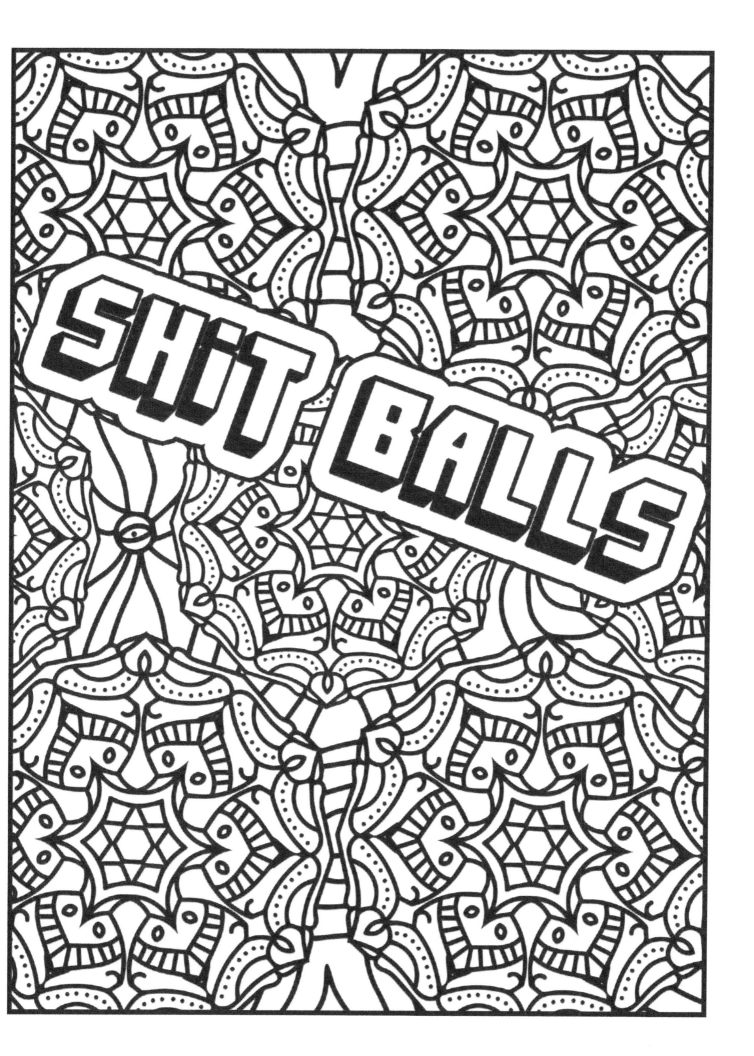

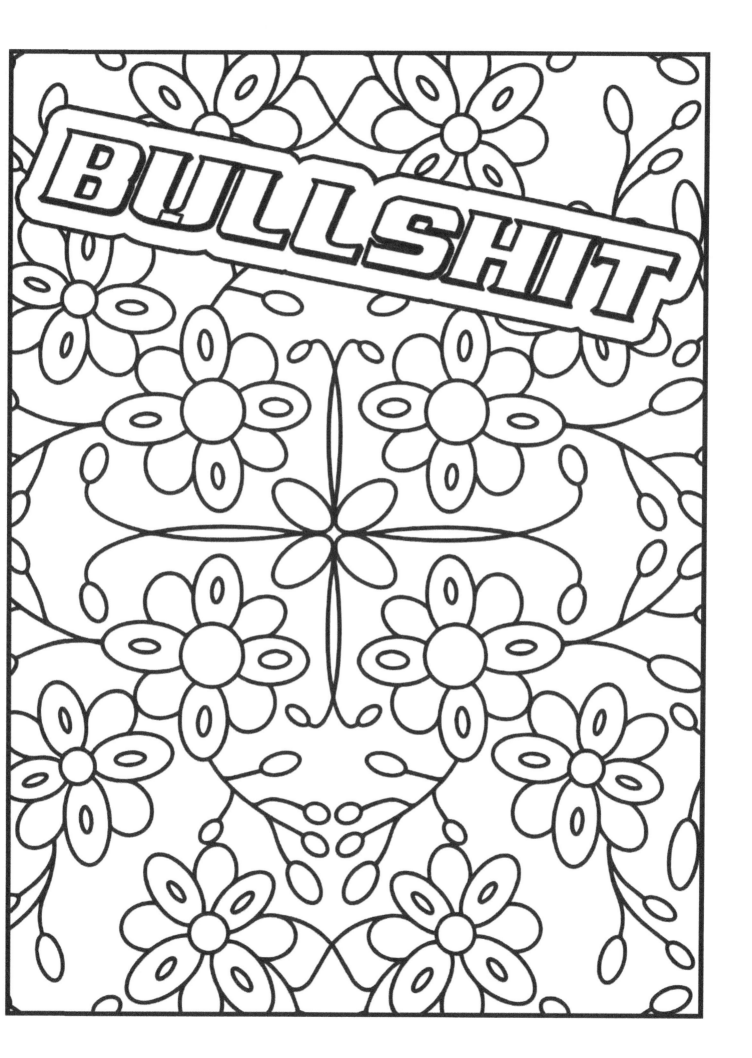

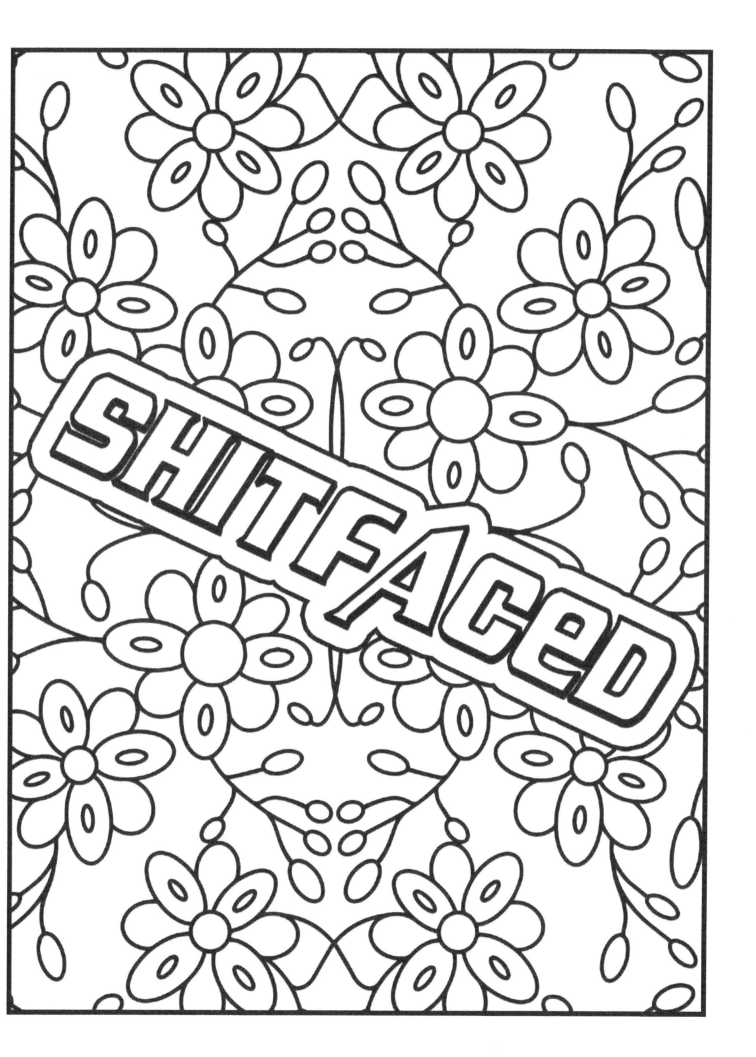

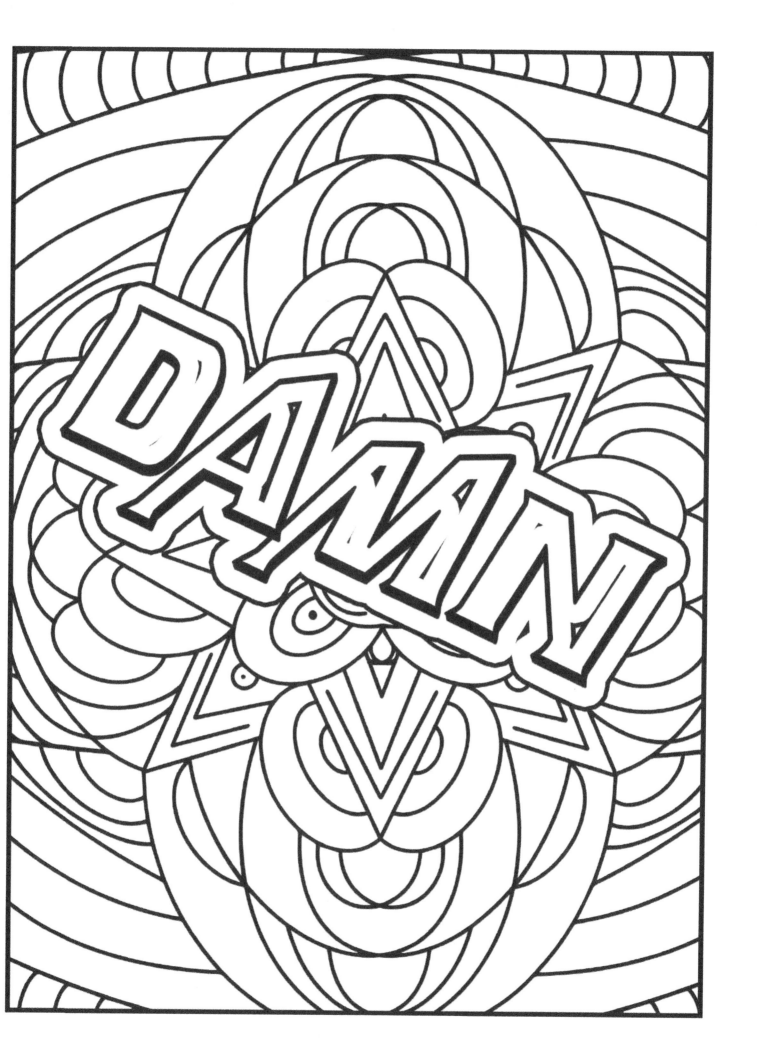

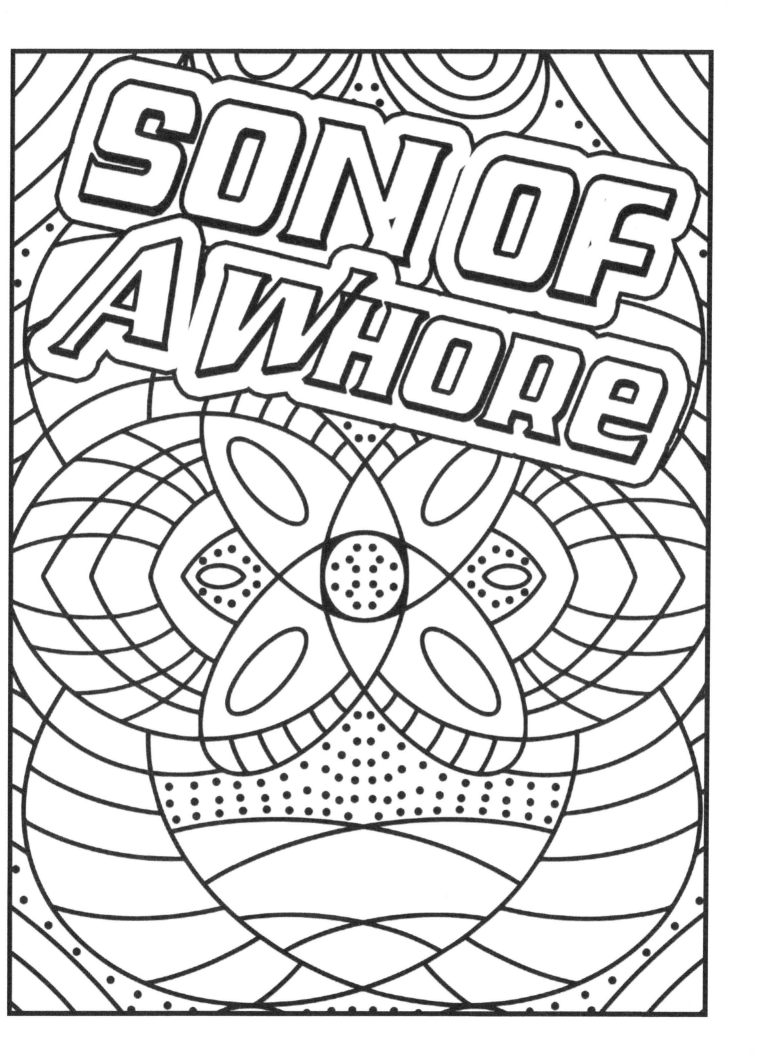

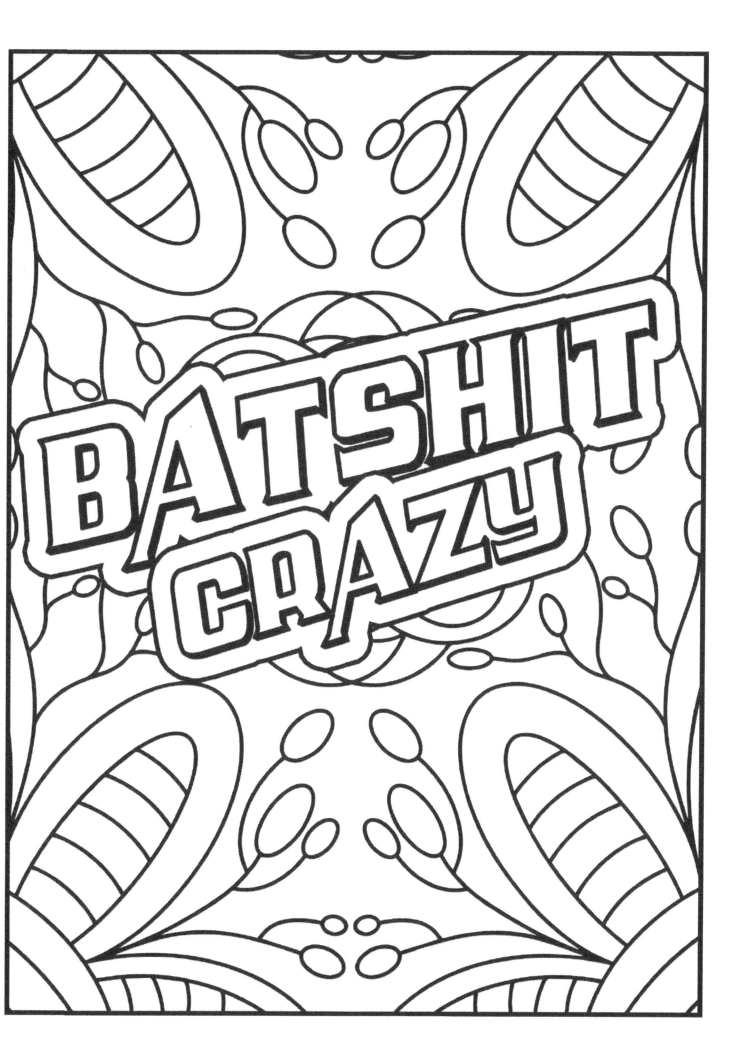

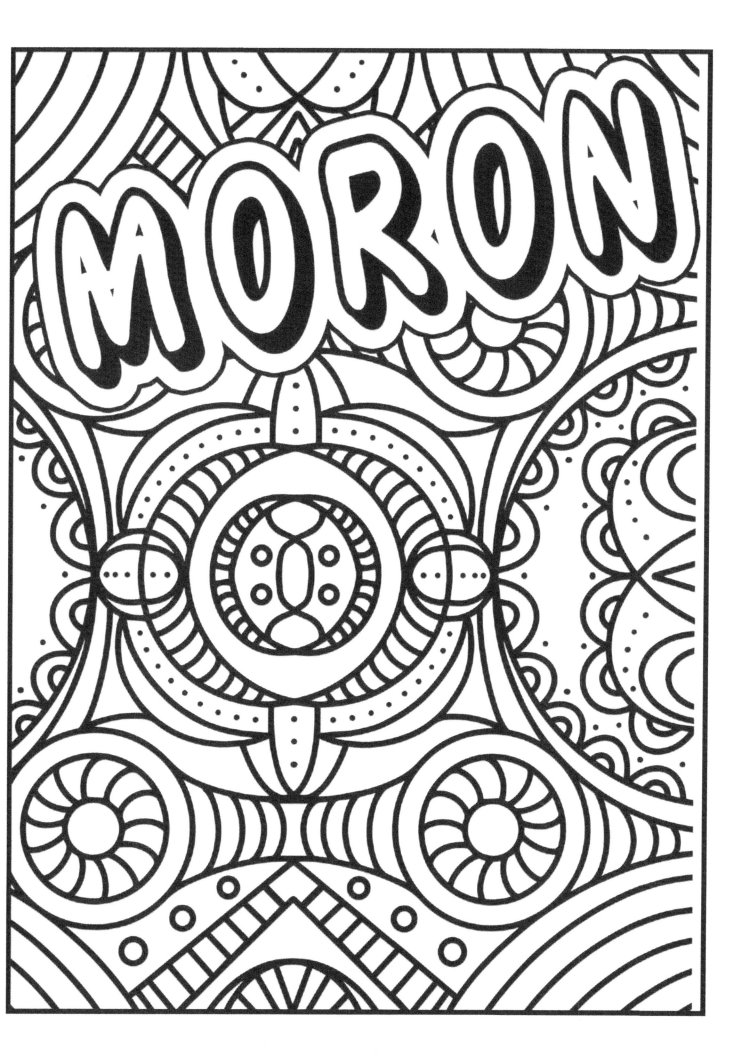

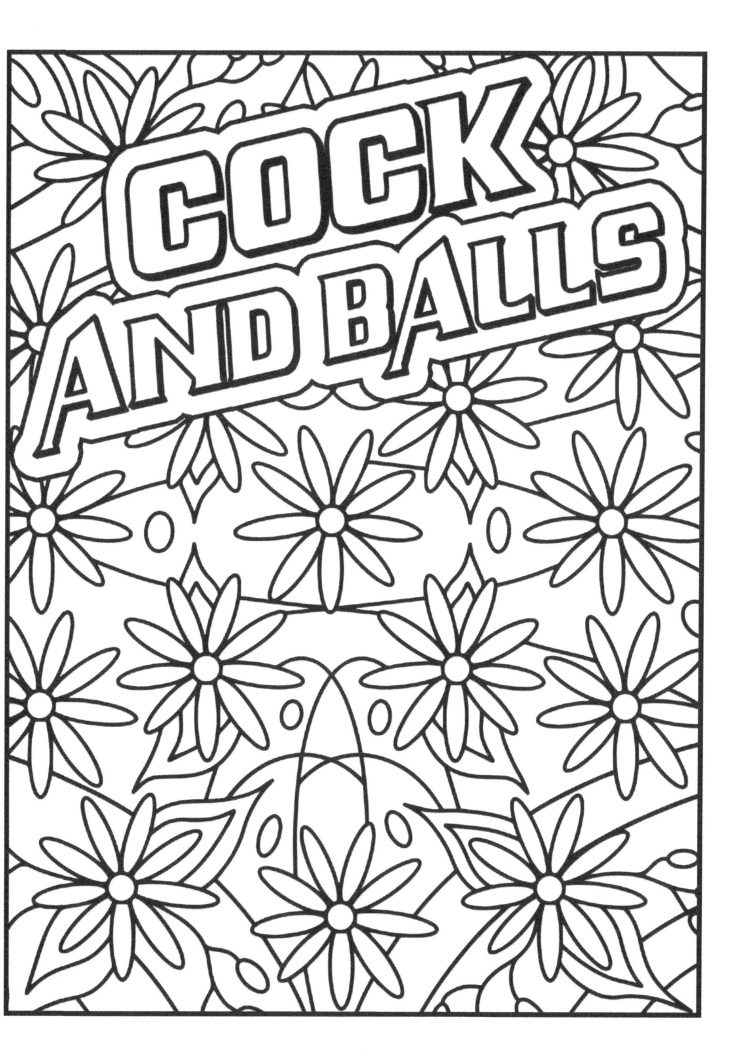

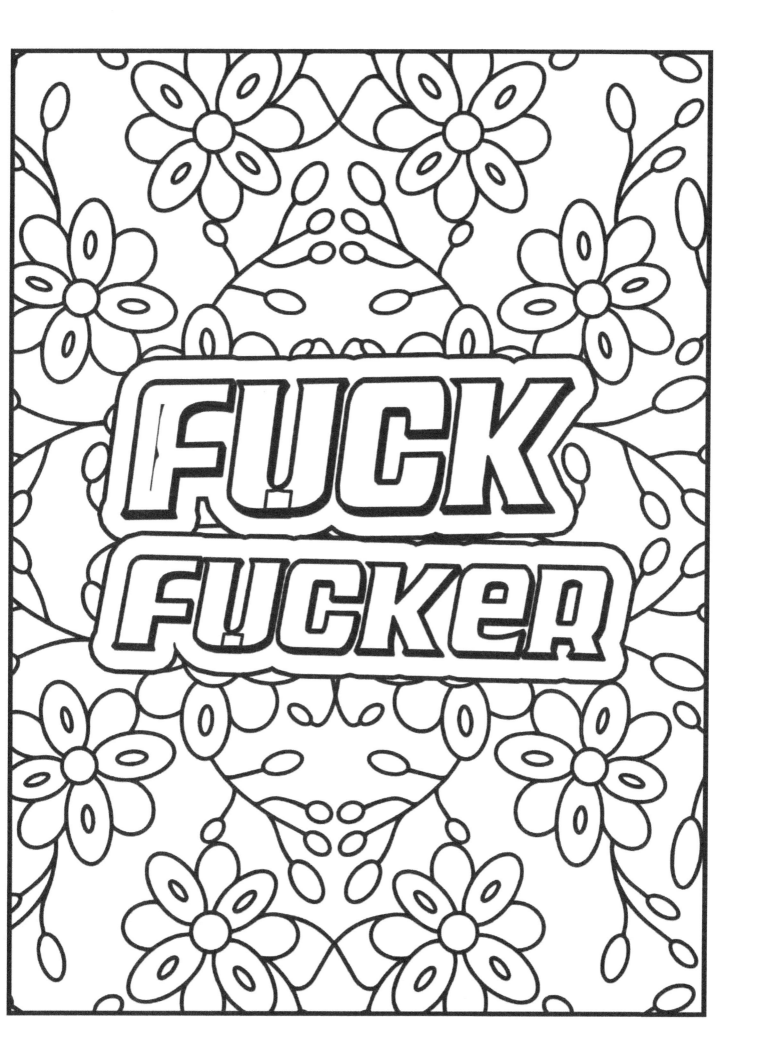

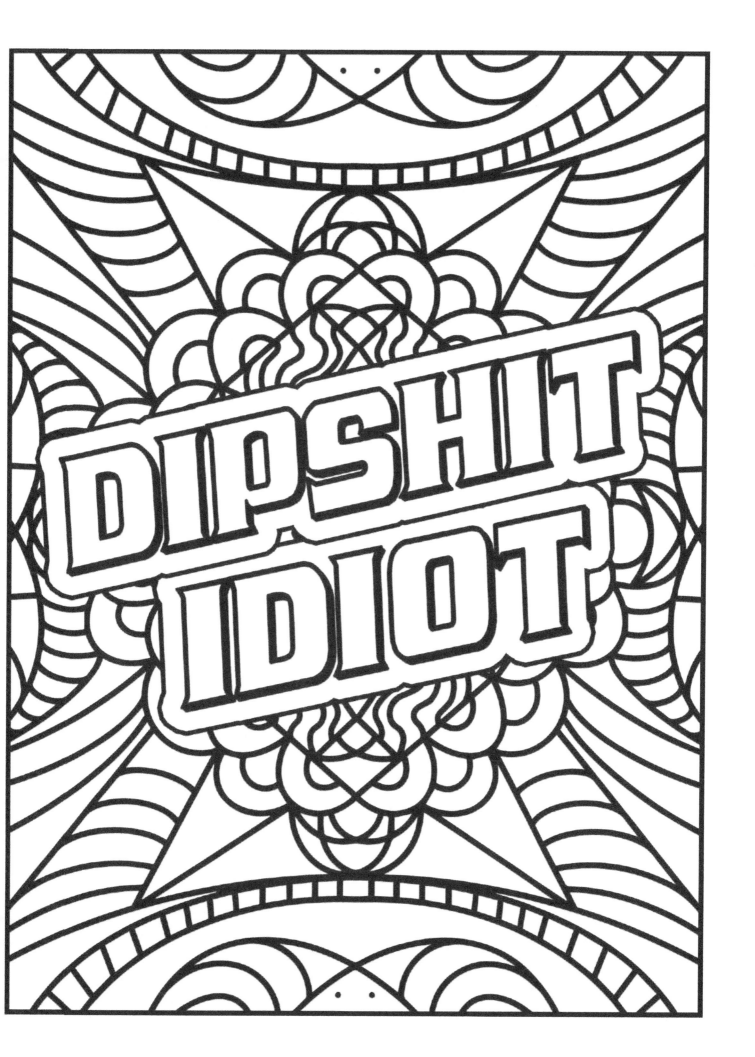

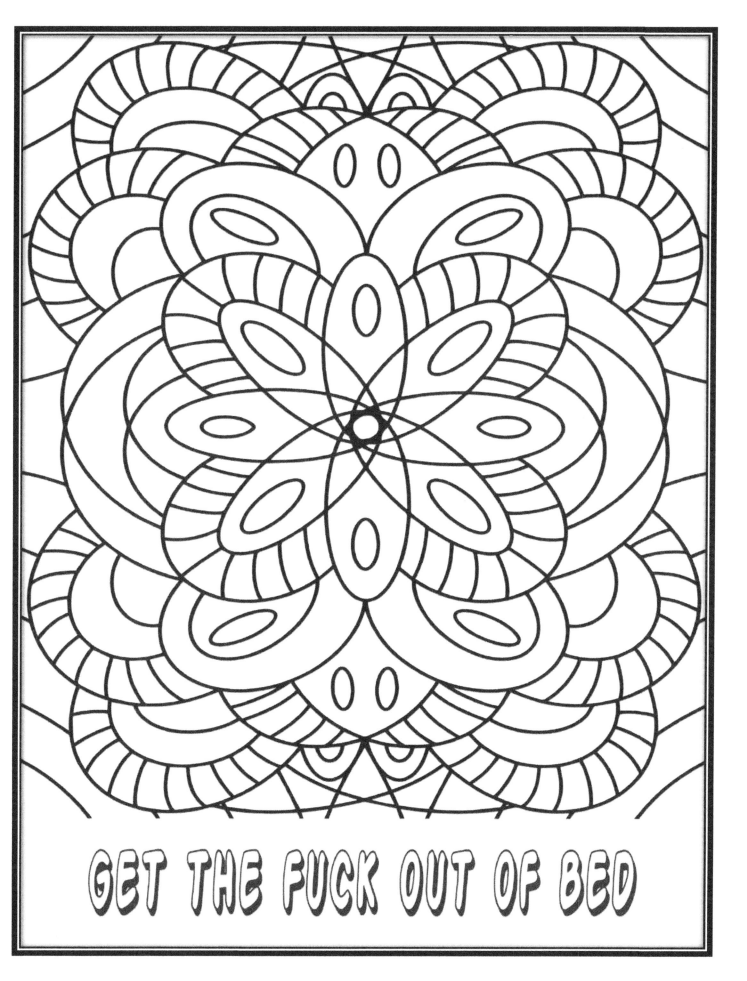

GET THE FUCK OUT OF BED

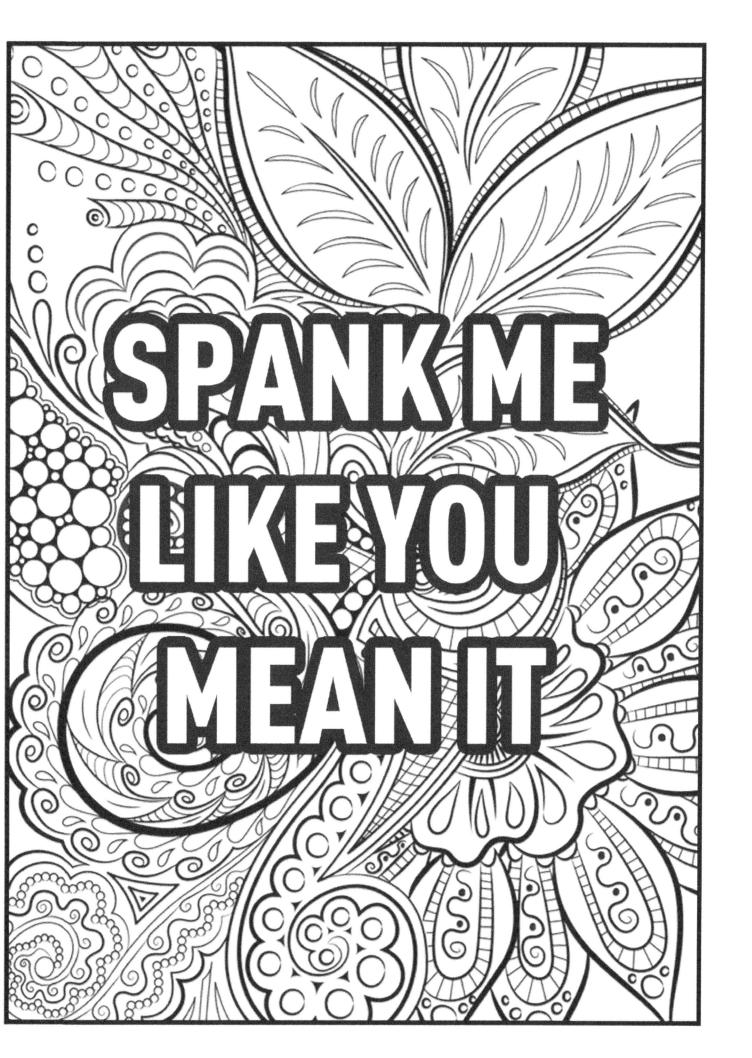

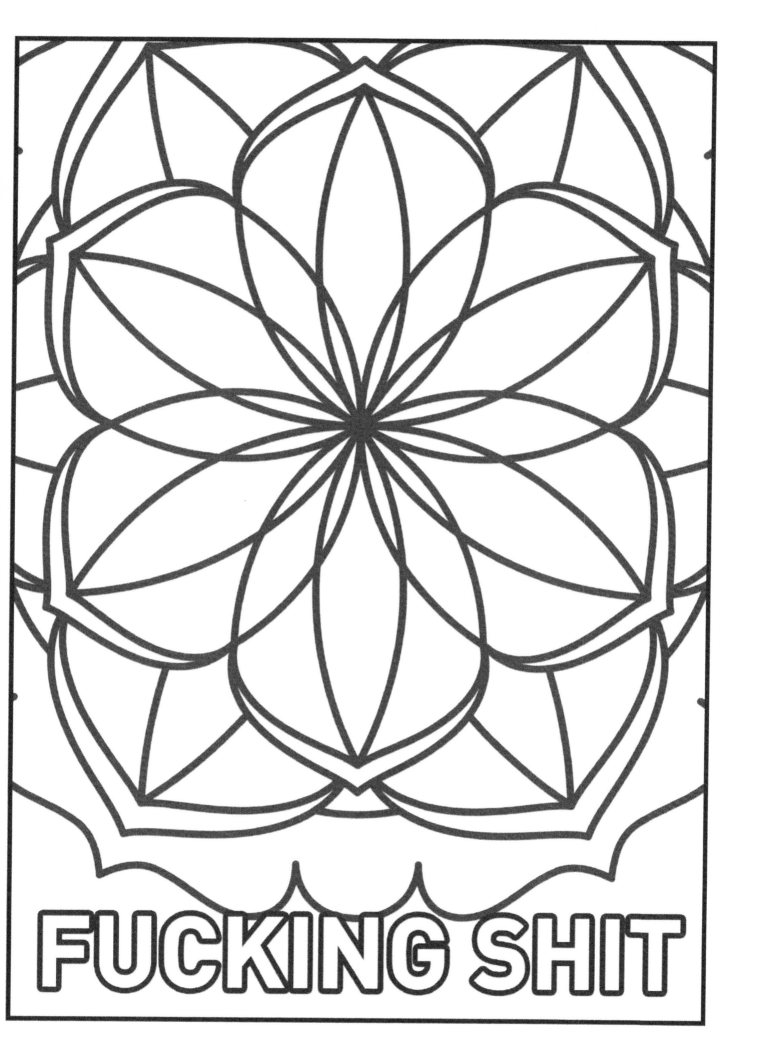

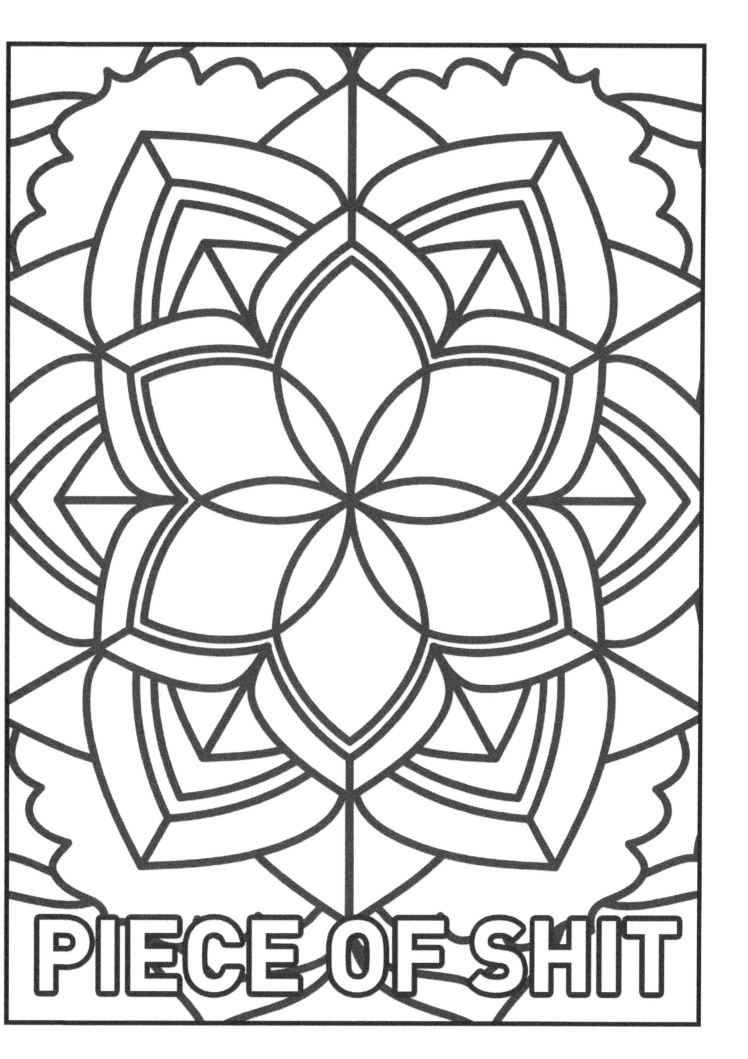

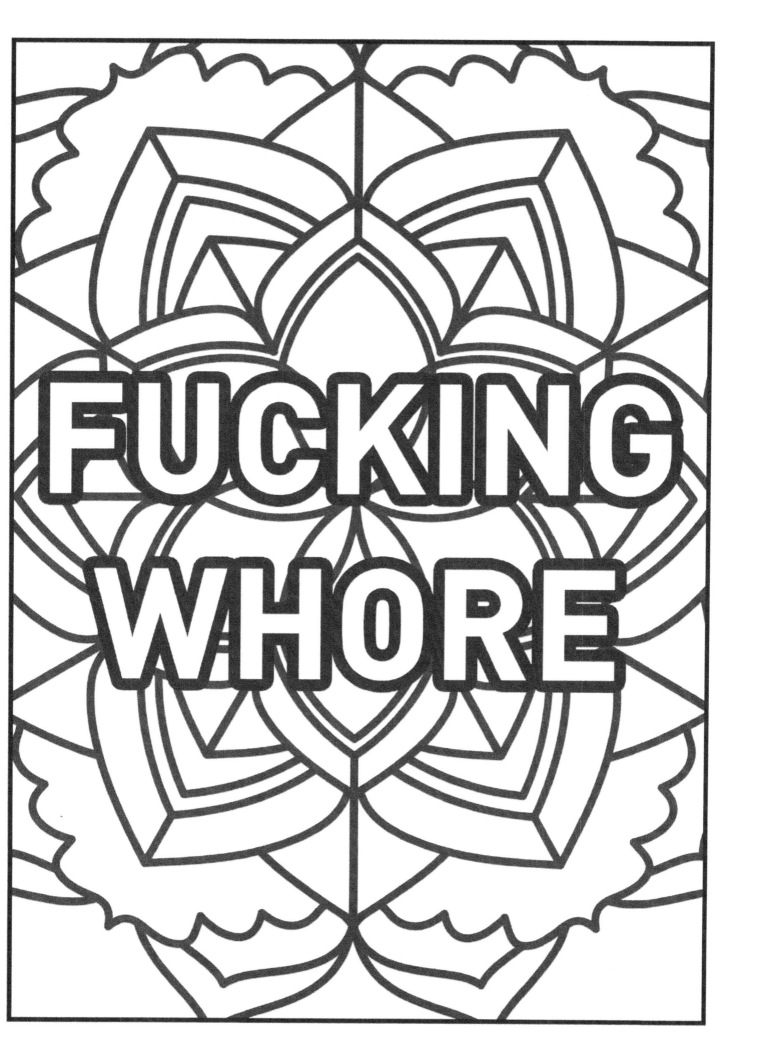

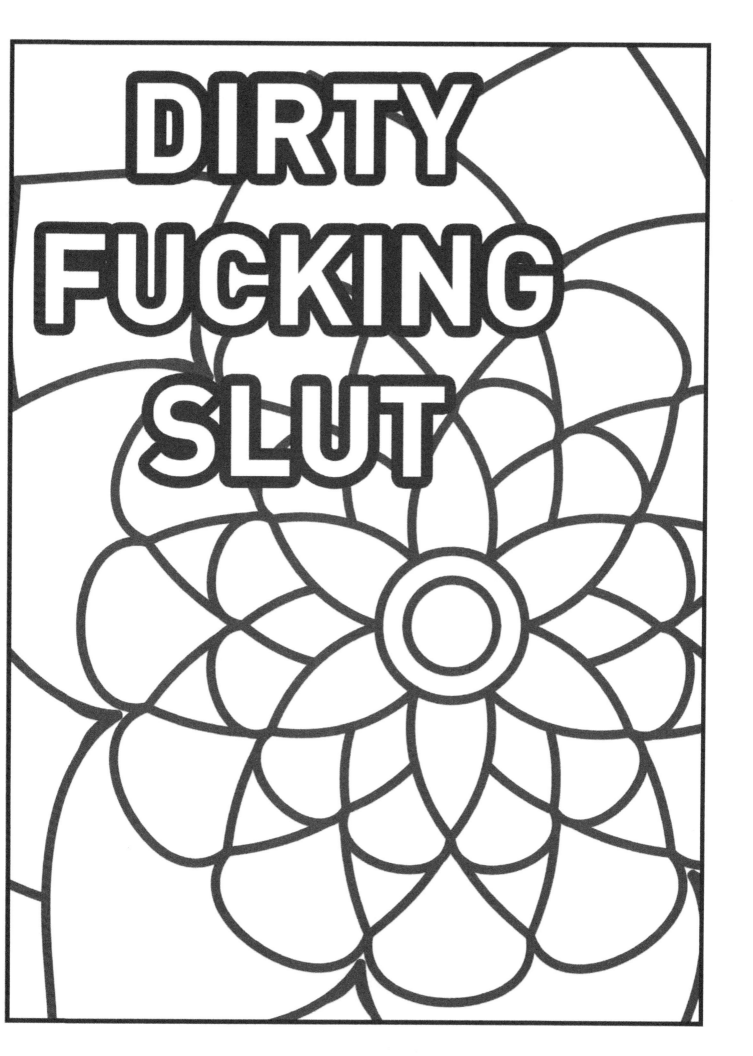

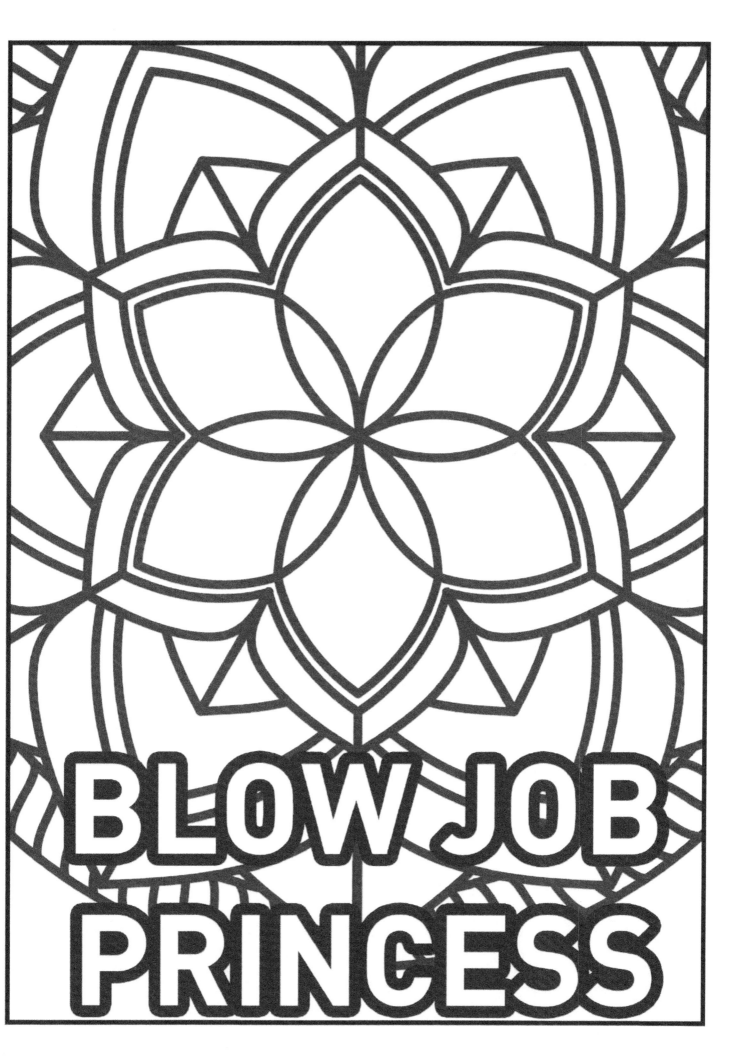

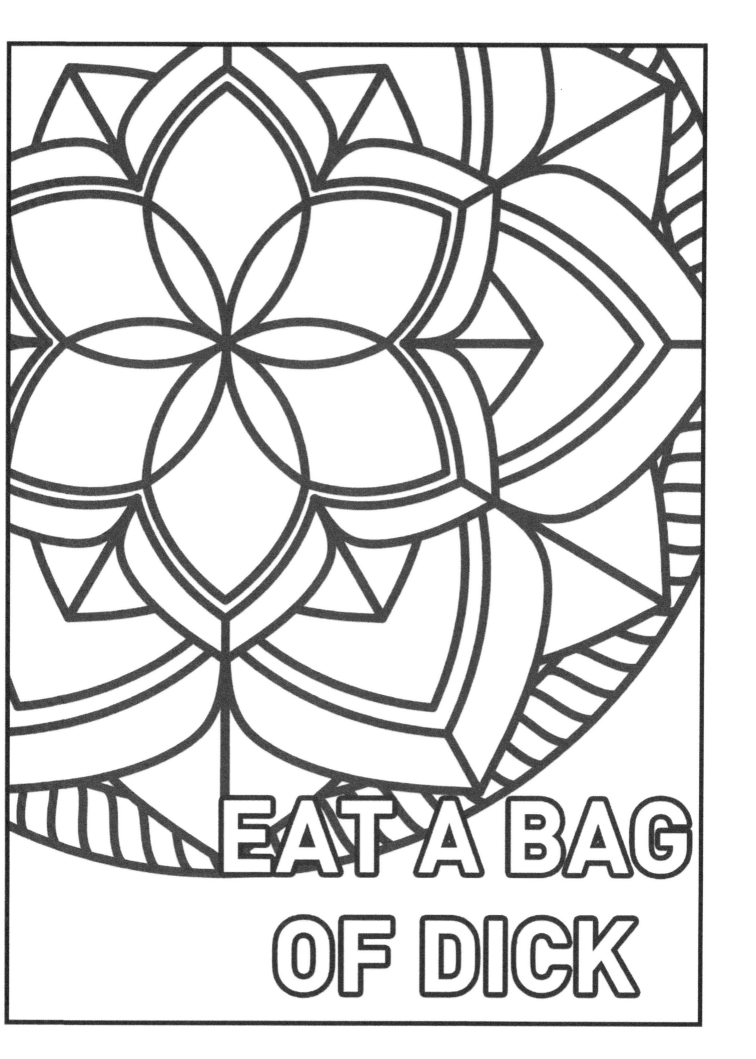

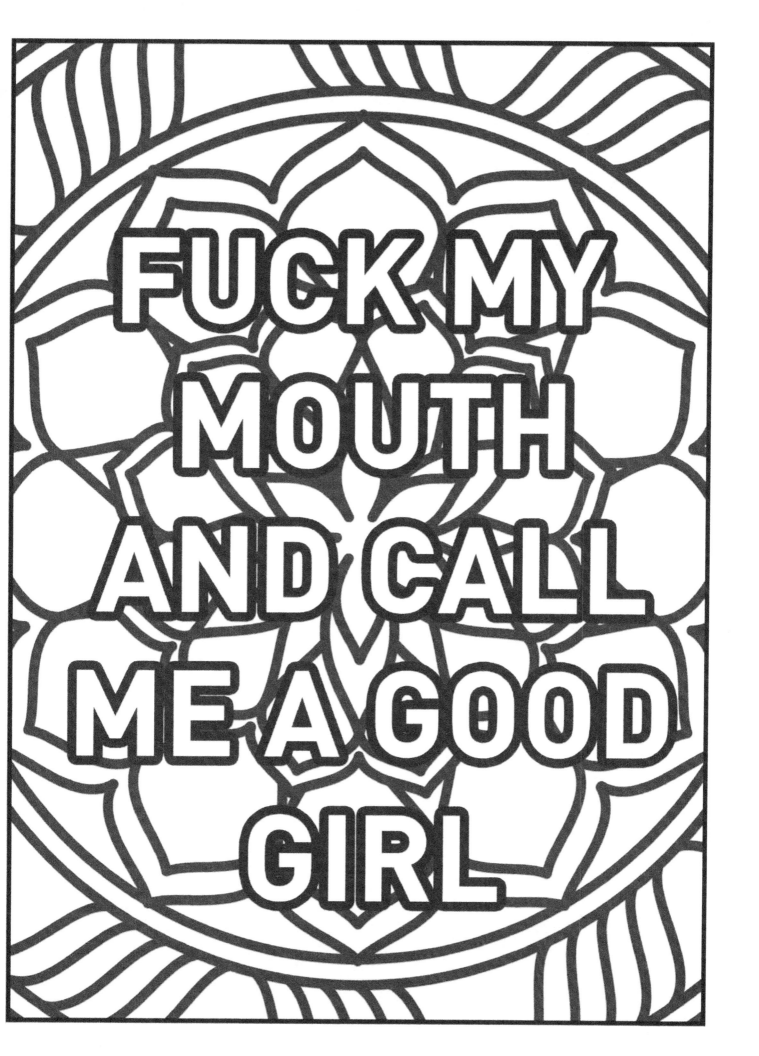

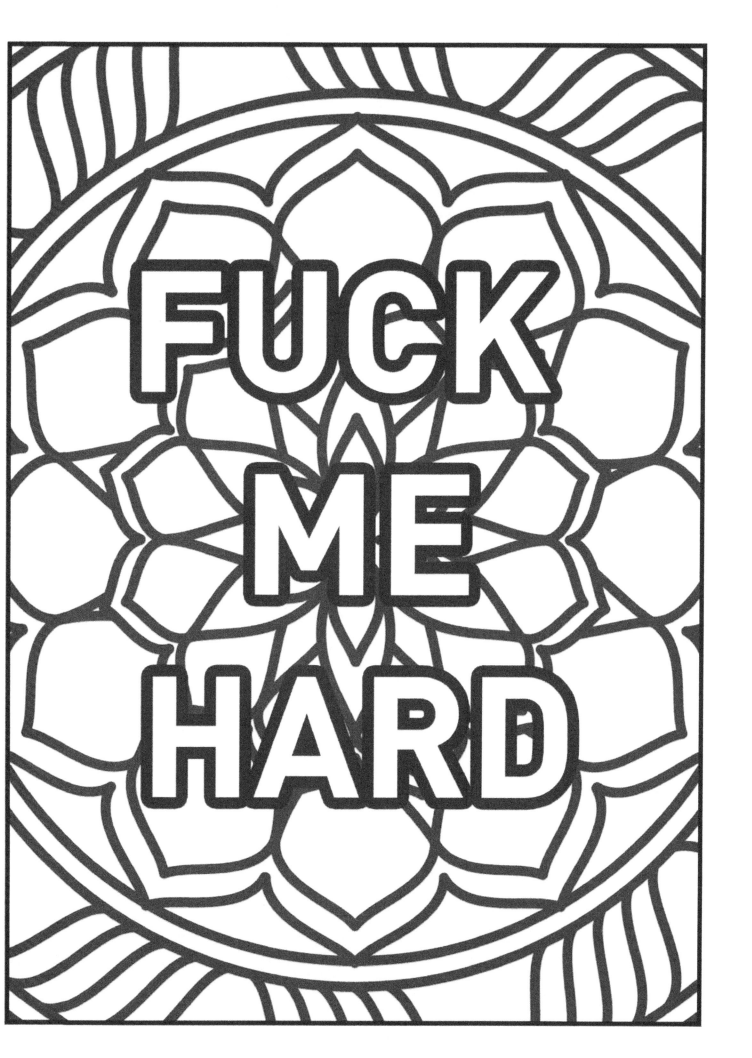

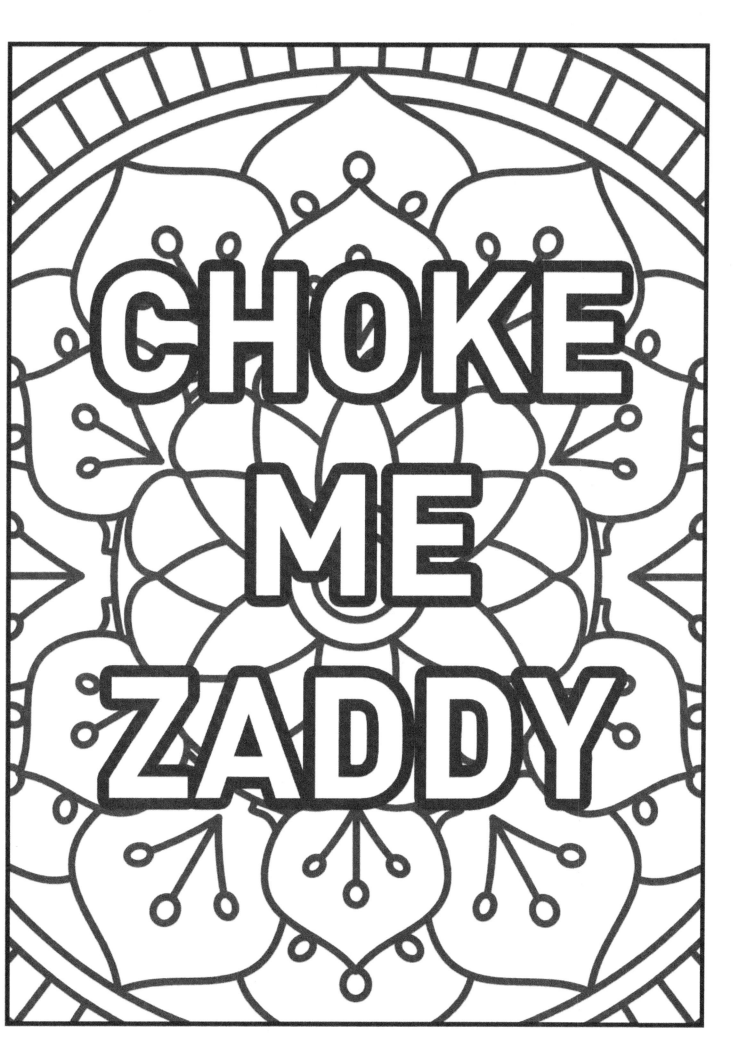

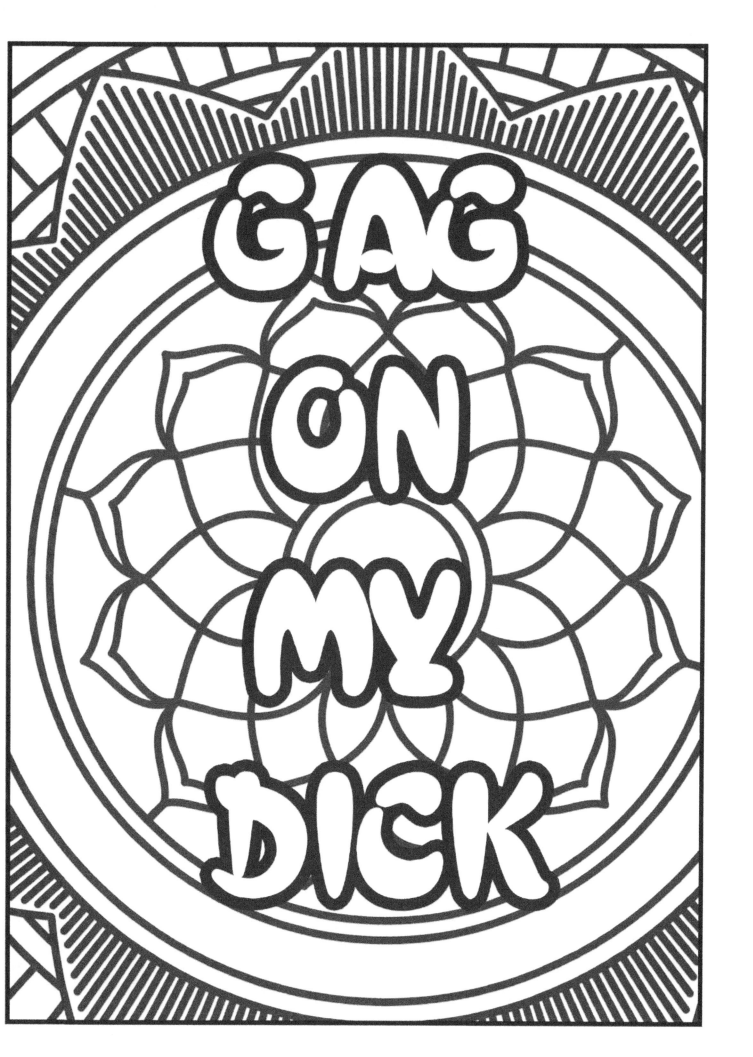

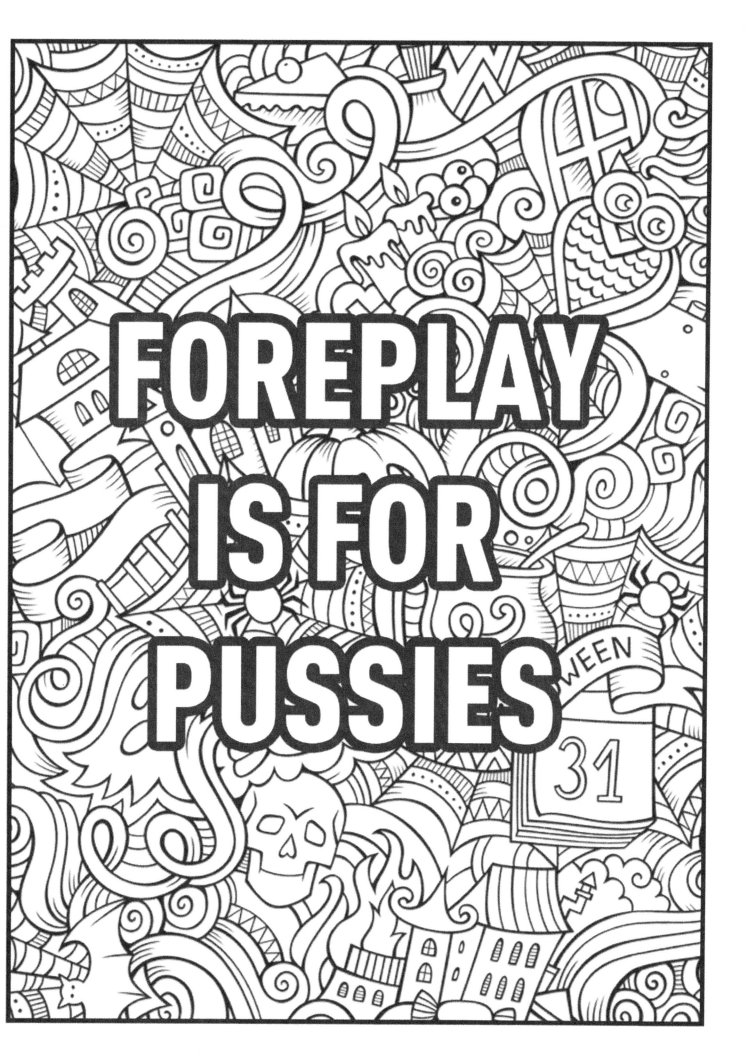

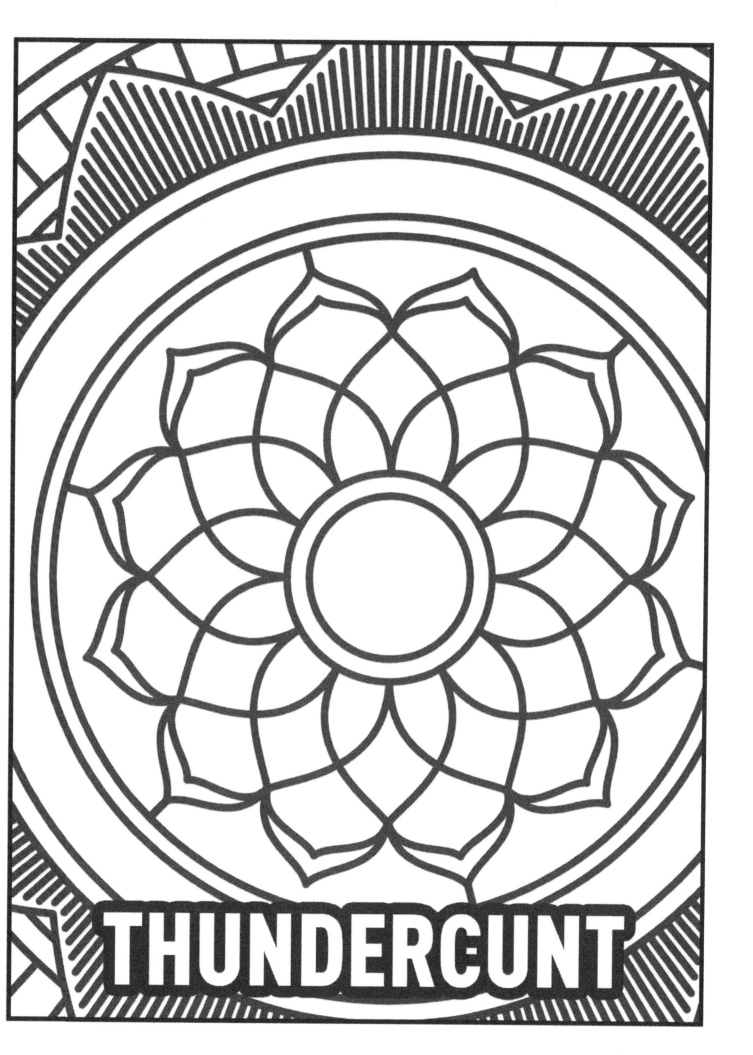

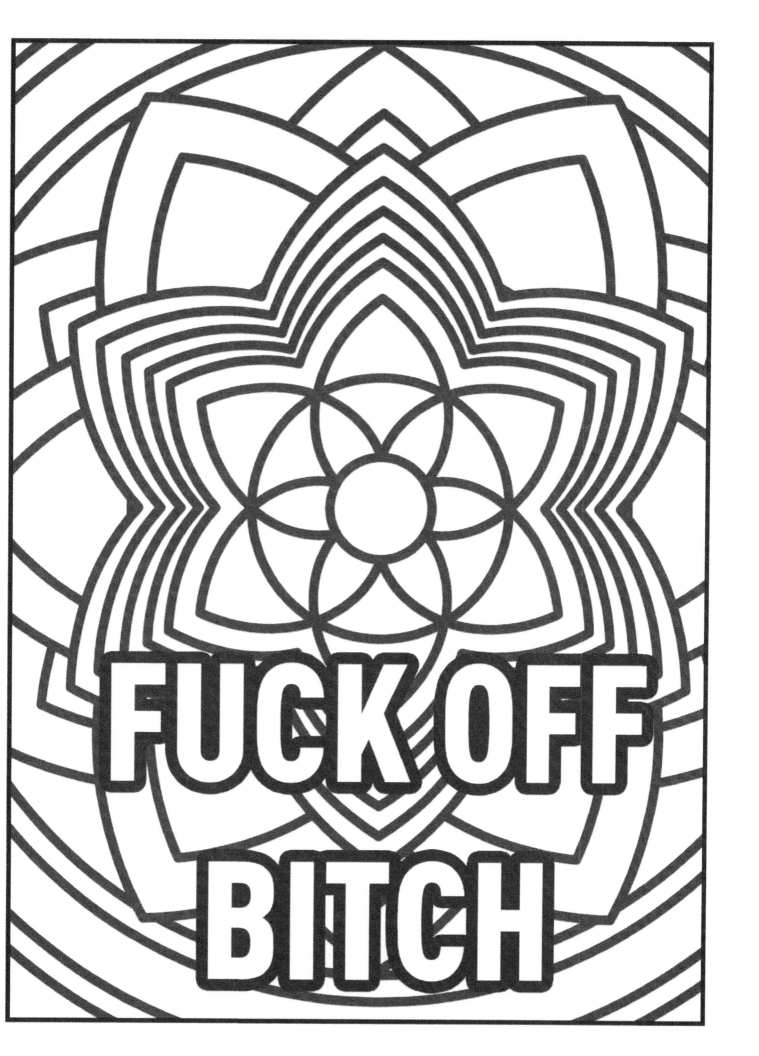

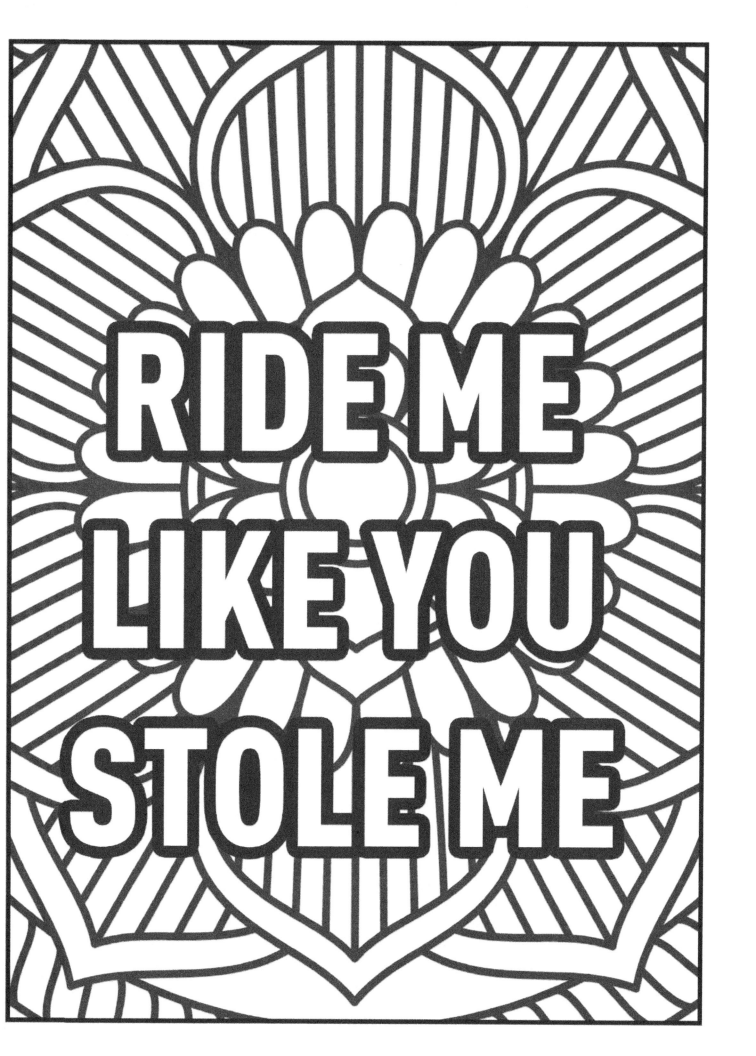

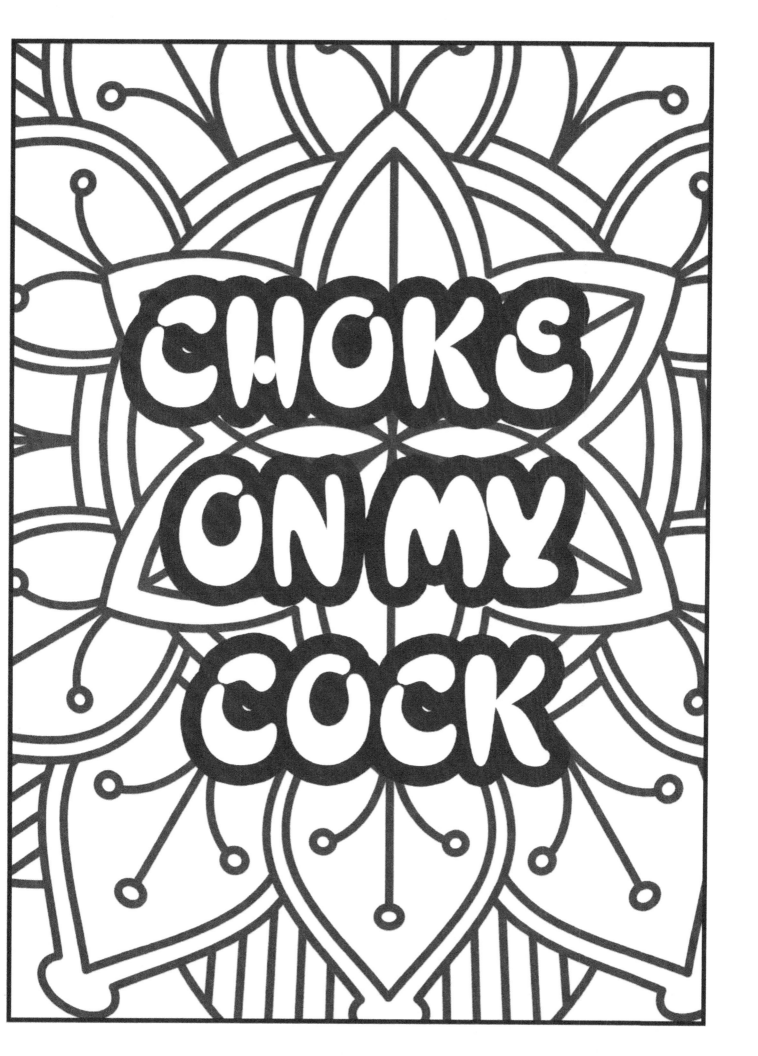

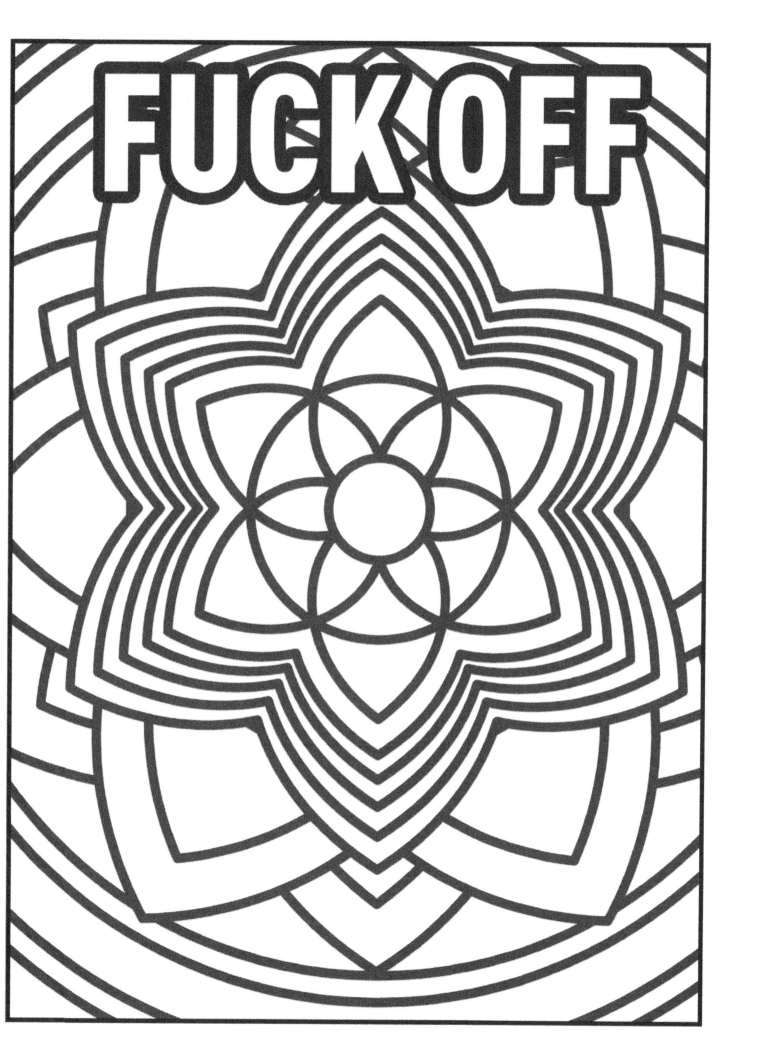

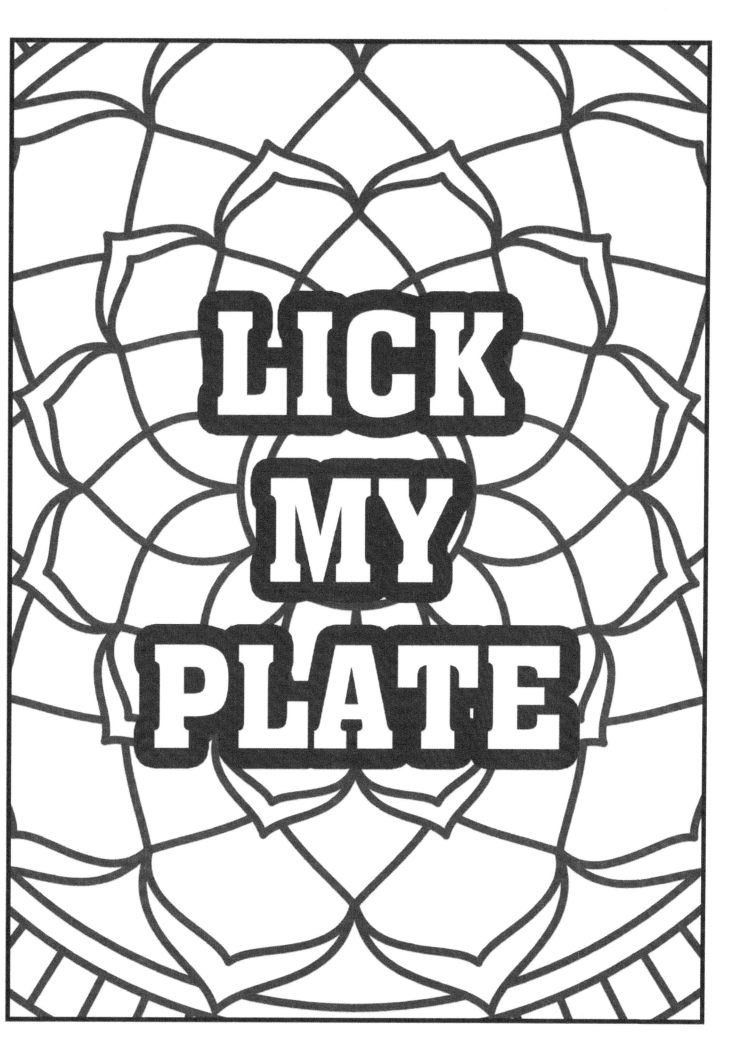

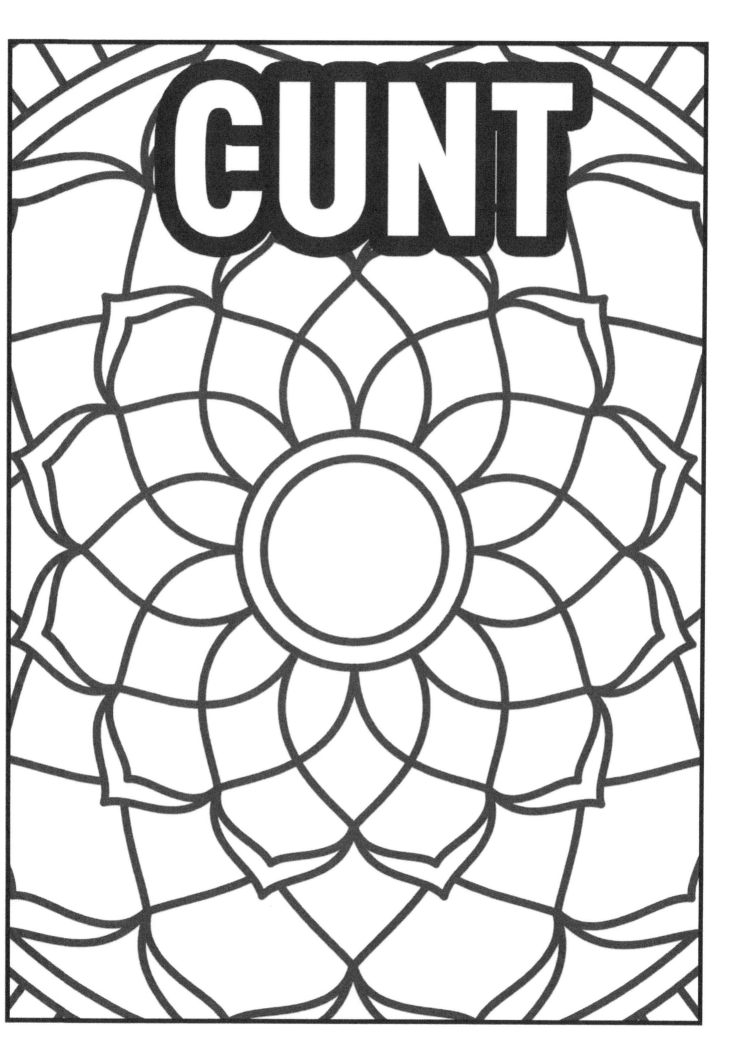

VAGITARIAN

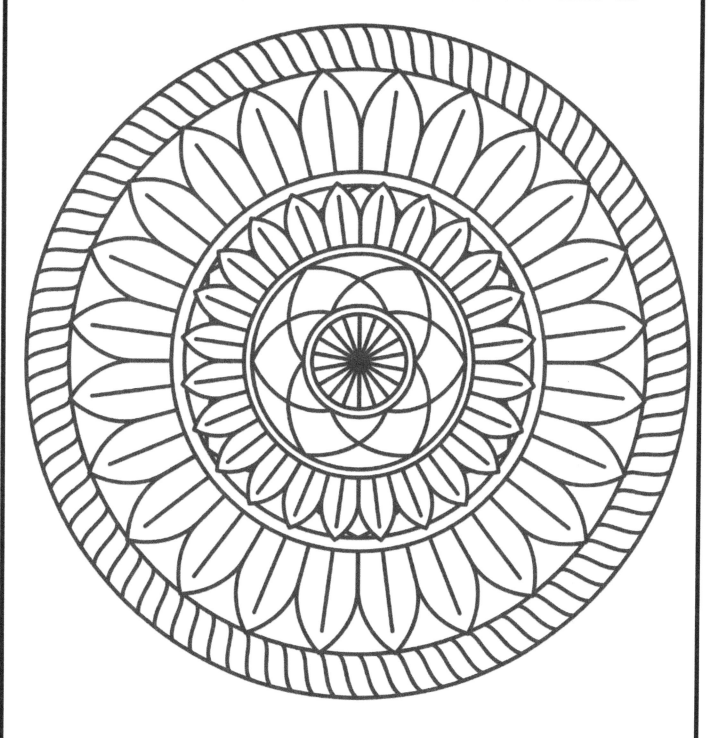

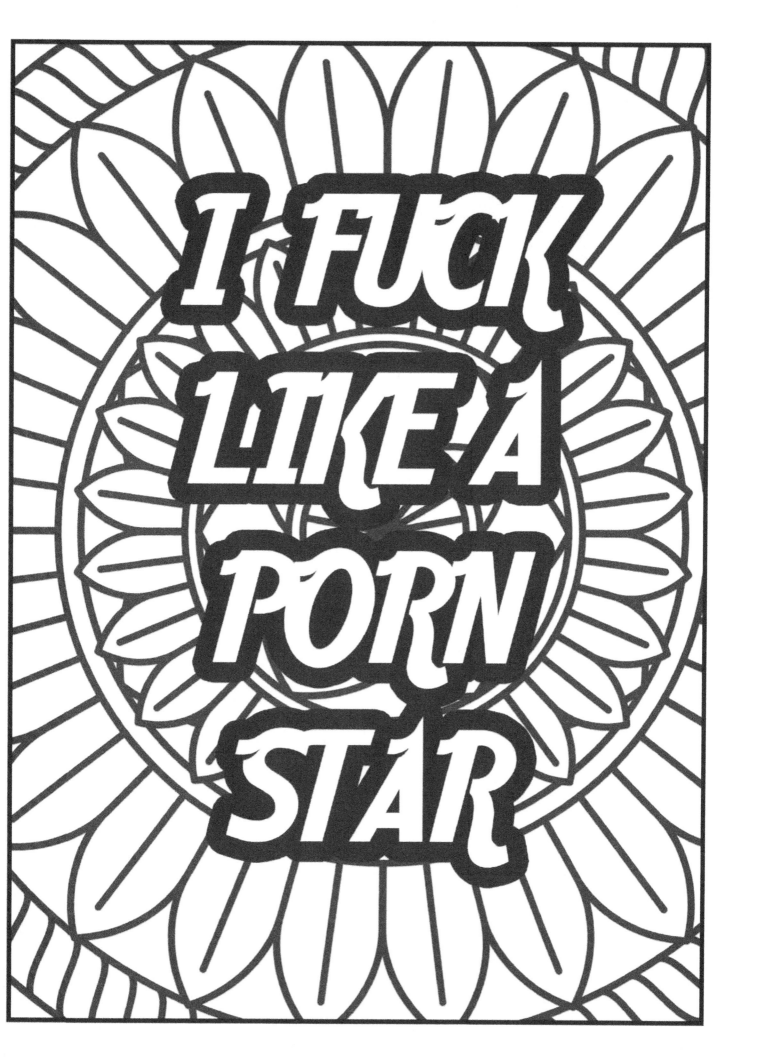

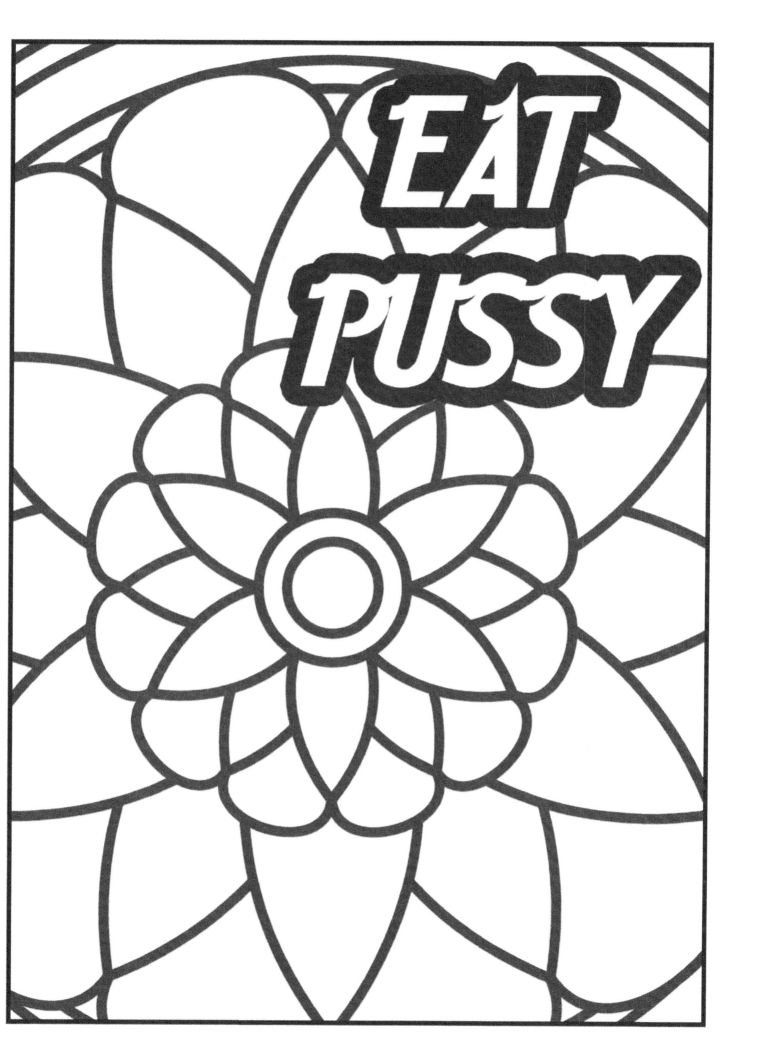

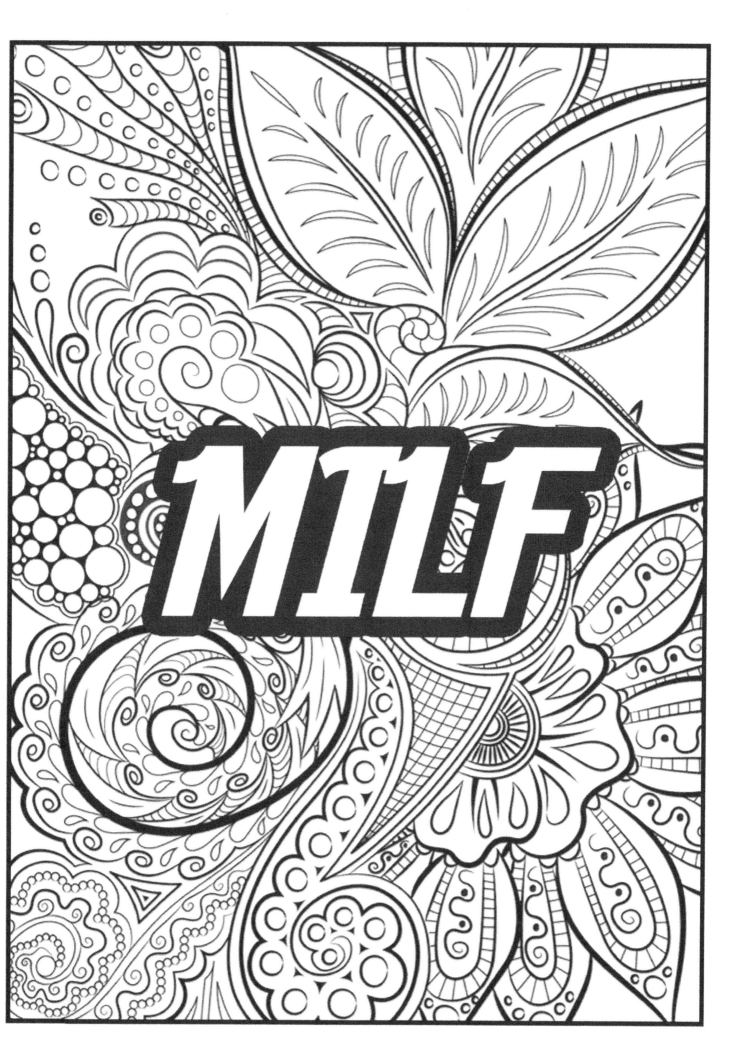

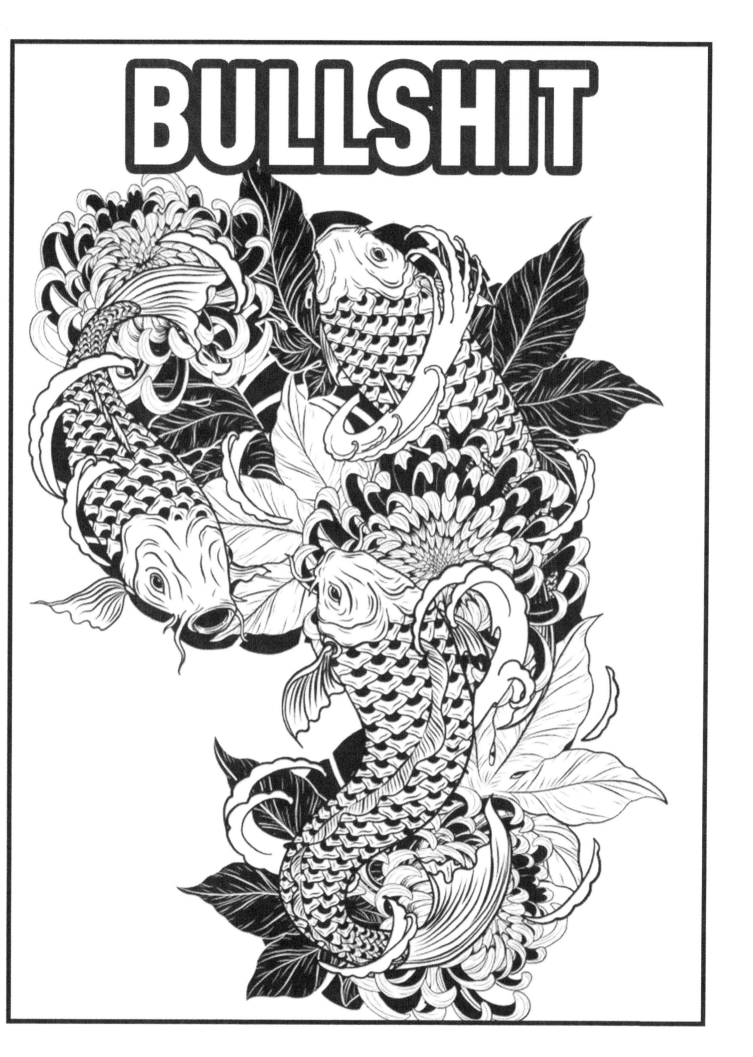

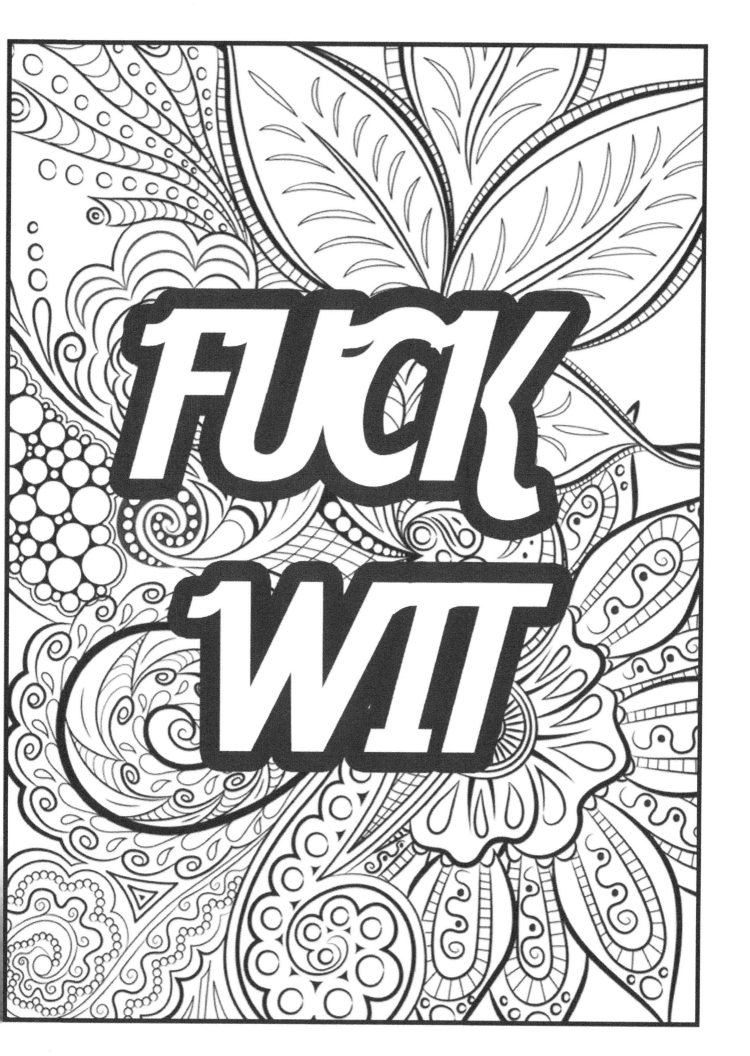

Made in the USA
Monee, IL
16 October 2023

44714294R00066